INTERNATIONAL CENTRE FOR MECHANICAL SCIENCES

COURSES AND LECTURES - No. 110

GIUSEPPE LONGO
UNIVERSITY OF TRIESTE

CODING FOR MARKOV SOURCES

COURSE HELD AT THE DEPARTMENT
FOR AUTOMATION AND INFORMATION
JUNE 1971

UDINE 1971

SPRINGER-VERLAG WIEN GMBH

Originally published by Springer-Verlag Wien New York in 1972

ISBN 978-3-211-81154-2 ISBN 978-3-7091-2961-6 (eBook)

DOI 10.1007/978-3-7091-2961-6

P R E F A C E

This course was given in June 1971 at the CISM in Udine. The notes, however, cover a wider material, since they include also the new results which I obtained later and presented at the Second International Symposium on Information Theory at Tsahkadsor in September, 1971.

The last Chapter is based entirely on those results and on further developments which will appear in the Proceedings of the sixth Prague Conference on Information Theory, held in September 1971.

J wish to thank the Italian Consiglio Nazionale delle Ricerche, Comitato Nazionale per le Scienze Matematiche for supporting the entire research as well as my travel to Tsahkadsor.

Udine, June 1971

P R E F A C E

These courses were given in June 1971 at the CISM in Udine. The notes, however, cover a wider material, since they include also the new results which I obtained lately and presented at the Second International Symposium on Information Theory, Tsahkadsor, in September 1971.

The last chapter [illegible] their results and further developments [illegible] appear in the Proceedings of the [illegible] Prague Conference [illegible] held in September 197[illegible].

I wish to thank [illegible] [illegible] [illegible] as well as [illegible].

[illegible]

Budapest, June [illegible]

Preliminaries.

Chapter 0

0.1. Introduction.

In this chapter we wish to summarize some fundamentals about finite Markov chains, which will be often used in the sequel.

Consider any system which can be found in k different states, s_1 , s_2 , ..., s_k , with a probability depending on the past history of the system. Assume that the system may change its current state only at discrete times:

$$\dots\ t_{-n}\ ,\ t_{-n+1}, \dots, t_{-1}, t_0, t_1, \dots, t_n, \dots \qquad (0.1)$$

The past history of the system is then the description of the particular sequence of states it has taken before the current instant, say t_0:

....

at time t_{-n} the system was in state $s_{i_{-n}}$

.... (0.2)

at time t_{-1} the system was in state $s_{i_{-1}}$

Once the past history of the system is given, we assume there is a well-defined probability for the system to be found at t_0 in any of its possible states:

(0.3) p_i = Prob (the system is in state s_i at t_0/given its history) $(1 \leq i \leq k)$

Of course the following are true

$$p_i \geq 0 \quad (1 \leq i \leq k) \quad \sum_{1}^{k} {}_i\, p_i = 1 . \tag{0.4}$$

It may happen that the influence of the past history on the probability for the system to be found in state s_i has a finite range, in the sense that only the last n states assumed, say $s_{i_{-n}}$, $s_{i_{-n+1}}$, ..., $s_{i_{-1}}$ influence p_i of (0.3). In other words if two past histories differ possibly only for some of the states assumed before time t_{-n}, then the corresponding conditional probabilities p_i coincide. In particular if $n = 1$, we say that our system has a Markov behaviour. Its past history has an influence on the probability of finding it in state s_i at time t_0 only in what it has led the system in state s_j at time t_{-1}. The history of such a system is called a "Markov chain", and any particular history in a realization of the Markov chain.

In the sequel only the conditional probabilities of a Markov chain, called "transition probabilities" will be important; these probabilities are of course defined as follows:

$$p_{ij} = \text{Prob (system in state } s_j \text{ at } t_0 | \text{ system in state } s_i \text{ at } t_{-1}) \tag{0.5}$$

and apparently they depend on the choice of the current time t_0. If this dependence actually does not exist, then we speak of a "stationary Markov chain" and (0.5) becomes:

$$p_{ij} = \text{Prob (system in state } s_j \text{ at } t_n | \text{system in state } s_i \text{ at } t_{n-1}) \quad n = \text{ any integer} \tag{0.6}$$

Since in (0.6) both indexes i and j range between 1 and k, there are k^2 transition probabilities, which can be arranged in a matrix Π :

$$\Pi = \begin{bmatrix} p_{11} & p_{12} & \cdots & p_{1k} \\ \cdots & \cdots & \cdots & \cdots \\ p_{k1} & p_{k2} & \cdots & p_{kk} \end{bmatrix} \tag{0.7}$$

Matrix Π above is called "the transition matrix" of the finite stationary Markov chain we are considering. Of course

$$p_{ij} \geqslant 0 \qquad (1 \leqslant i, j \leqslant k) \tag{0.8}$$

and since from any state s_i a transition to some state s_j is necessary, also:

$$\sum_{1}^{k}{}_j \, p_{ij} = 1 \qquad (1 \leqslant i \leqslant k) \tag{0.9}$$

Properties (0.8) and (0.9) are briefly accounted for by saying that Π is a "stochastic matrix".

If we think of starting the chain at a given initial time, t_0 say, we must add a kind of "initial probability distribution" ruling the initial state; let Π_0 be this initial distribution, and put

$$\Pi_0 = \begin{bmatrix} p_1 & p_2 & \dots & p_k \end{bmatrix} \tag{0.10}$$

Remark that in particular Π_0 can be taken as a degenerate p.d.(*), i.e. it can contain $k-1$ zeroes and one 1.

0.2. Higher order transitions.

Let $p_{ij}^{(n)}$ be the probability of finding the Markov chain in state s_j at time t_m given it was in state s_i at time t_{m-n} (m , n positive integers). By (0.6) we have for $n = 1$

$$p_{ij}^{(1)} = p_{ij} \tag{0.11}$$

while for $n = 2$

$$p_{ij}^{(2)} = \sum_{1}^{k}{}_{\ell}\, p_{i\ell}\, p_{\ell j} \tag{0.12}$$

and in general

$$p_{ij}^{(n+1)} = \sum_{1}^{k}{}_{\ell}\, p_{i\ell}\, p_{\ell j}^{(n)} . \tag{0.13}$$

(*) In the sequel p.d. will mean probability distribution.

Expression (0.13) can be further generalized as follows:

$$p_{ij}^{(n+m)} = \sum_{1}^{k} {}_{\ell}\; p_{i\ell}^{(n)}\; p_{\ell j}^{(m)} \tag{0.14}$$

If $p_{ij}^{(n)}$ is considered as the (i , j)-th entry of a square matrix $\Pi^{(n)}$ of type k , equations (0.11) to (0.14) can be rewritten in terms of the successive powers of matrix Π , the product being performed as usual rows by columns:

$$\Pi^{(1)} = \Pi \tag{0.11'}$$

$$\Pi^{(2)} = \Pi^{2} \tag{0.12'}$$

$$\Pi^{(n+1)} = \Pi \cdot \Pi^{n} \tag{0.13'}$$

$$\Pi^{(n+m)} = \Pi^{n} \cdot \Pi^{m} \tag{0.14'}$$

We remark explicitly that for any positive integer n , Π^{n} is a stochastic matrix if Π is.

0.3. Closed state sets.

Let $\mathcal{A} = \{ s_1, s_2, \ldots, s_k \}$ be the set of all the states of a stationary Markov chain. Then a set $\mathcal{C} \subset \mathcal{A}$ is called "closed" if starting from a state in $\mathcal{C}$, no state outside $\mathcal{C}$ can ever be reached. Of course $\mathcal{A}$ itself is a closed state set.

Given any $\mathcal{D} \subset \mathcal{A}$, the smallest closed set containing $\mathcal{S}$ is called the "closure" of $\mathcal{S}$.

A single state s_i is said "absorbing" if $\{s_i\}$ is a closed set.

From the above definitions and from n. 2 it is easily seen that:

- $\mathcal{C}$ is closed iff $p_{ij}^{(n)} = 0$ for $s_i \in \mathcal{C}$, $s_j \notin \mathcal{C}$ and each $n = 1,2,\dots$
- By eliminating from Π^n the rows and columns corresponding to the states outside $\mathcal{C}$ one gets a new stochastic matrix ($n = 1,2,\dots$), whose composition laws are again (0.11) - (0.14).
- s_i is absorbing iff $p_{ii} = 1$.

If $\mathcal{C}$ is a closed state set and $\mathcal{C} \neq \mathcal{A}$, the corresponding chain is said to be "reducible". Once the chain enters $\mathcal{C}$ it never gets out.

Conversely a chain is called "irreducible" if no set $\mathcal{C} \subsetneqq \mathcal{A}$ is closed. As a consequence

- A chain is irreducible iff every state can be reached from every state.

The complementary $\mathcal{A} - \mathcal{C}$ of a closed set $\mathcal{C}$ is not necessarily closed. A closed set $\mathcal{C}$ can be further reducible, i.e. it may contain smaller closed sets $\mathcal{C}'$, $\mathcal{C}''$, ...

0.4. Classification of states.

A state s_i is called "periodic of period t"

($t > 1$) if $p_{ii}^{(n)} = 0$ unless n is a multiple of t , and t is the smallest integer having this property.

A state s_i for which such a $t > 1$ does not exist is called "aperiodic".

The following definitions are useful for classifying aperiodic states: let

$$b_{ij}^{(n)} \geqslant 0 \qquad \left(n = 1,2,\ldots; \ b_{ij}^{(0)} = 0\right) \tag{0.15}$$

be the probability that starting from s_i one reaches s_j for the first time at step n . Let

$$b_{ij} = \sum_{1}^{\infty} {}_n \, b_{ij}^{(n)} \tag{0.16}$$

be the probability that starting from s_i one eventually reaches s_j . Of course

$$b_{ij} \leqslant 1 \tag{0.17}$$

and if $b_{ij} = 1$, then the sequence $\left\{ b_{ij}^{(n)} \right\}$ is a denumerable probability distribution (probability distribution of the first passage through s_j).

Set now $j = i$ in (0.15) - (0.17); if

$$b_{ij} = 1 \tag{0.18}$$

then the sequence $\left\{ b_{ii}^{(n)} \right\}$ is called the "p.d. of the recurrence times for s_i ". If (0.18) is true, then the quantity

$$\mu_i = \sum_{1}^{\infty} n \, n \, b_{ii}^{(n)} \tag{0.19}$$

is called the "mean recurrence time" for state s_i .

The aperiodic states of a Markov chain can now be classified as follows:

- A state s_i is called "persistent" if $b_{ii} = 1$ (cf. (0.16)); if $b_{ii} < 1$, s_i is called "transient"
- A persistent state s_i is called "null" if $\mu_i = \infty$ (cf. (0.19)); if μ_i is finite, s_i is called "ergodic."

We state without proof some very important theorems (*):

Theorem 0.1 - All the states of an irreducible chain are of the same type; i.e. either they are all periodic of the same period, or they are all aperiodic; in the latter case they are all transient or all persistent, and in the latter case either all the states are null or all ergodic.

Theorem 0.2 - Given a persistent state s_i , there exists a unique irreducible closed set $\mathcal{C} \ni s_i$ such that for every pair s_j, s_k of states in $\mathcal{C}$ one has

$$b_{ik} = 1 , \qquad b_{kj} = 1 .$$

(*) These theorems refer to Markov chains having a denumerable infinity of states; we shall see how they change for finite chains.

In other words, once in $\mathcal{C}$ the process does not get out and passes through every state in $\mathcal{C}$.

Theorem 0.3 - The states of a Markov chain can be partitioned, in a unique way, into a family of disjoint sets:

$$\mathcal{A} = \mathcal{T} \cup \mathcal{C}_1 \cup \mathcal{C}_2 \cup \ldots \qquad (0.20)$$

such that $\mathcal{T}$ contains all transient states, $\mathcal{C}_i\,(i = 1,2,\ldots)$ is a set of persistent states and if $s_j \in \mathcal{C}_i$, then $b_{jk} = 1$ for $s_k \in \mathcal{C}_i$, $b_{jk} = 0$ for $s_k \notin \mathcal{C}_i$. In each $\mathcal{C}_i$ the states are all of the same type (i.e. either null or ergodic).

Theorem 0.4 - A finite chain has no null states and it is impossible that all the states are transient.

0.5. Stationary distributions.

It is very important to investigate on the limiting behaviour of the higher order transition probabilities, defined in § 0.2. One important result is known about "ergodic" chains, i.e. irreducible chains whose states are all ergodic, i.e. aperiodic persistent and non null. Actually the following theorem is true:

Theorem 0.5 - If an irreducible Markov chain is ergodic, the limits

$$w_i = \lim_{n \to \infty} p_{ji}^{(n)} \qquad (1 \leq i \leq k) \qquad (0.21)$$

exist and do not depend on the initial state s_j. Moreover

(0.22) $$w_i > 0 \,, \quad \sum_1^k{}_i \; w_i = 1$$

and

(0.23) $$w_i = \sum_1^k{}_j \; w_j \, p_{ji} \,.$$

Expressions (0.22) tell us that the row-vector

(0.24) $$W = \begin{bmatrix} w_1 & w_2 & \dots & w_k \end{bmatrix}$$

represents a probability distribution, which is called "stationary" due to (0.21). In matrix form (0.23) becomes

(0.25) $$W = W\Pi$$

where definitions (0.7) and (0.24) have been used. By (0.23) or (0.25) the stationary p.d. W is an invariant p.d. The following converse theorem is also true:

Theorem 0.6 - If there exist K nonnegative numbers $w_1, w_2, \dots w_k$ satisfying (0.22) and (0.23), being the p_{ji} the entries of the transition matrix of an irriducible aperiodic Markov chain, then the chain is ergodic, the numbers w_i are given by the limits (0.21) and moreover

(0.26) $$w_i = \frac{1}{\mu_i}$$

being μ_i the mean ricurrence time of state s_i. As a consequence of this theorem, there is a unique invariant p.d. for an irreducible ergodic chain, and this invariant p.d. is of course the stationary p.d.

Let $\Pi_0 = [p_1 \; p_2 \; \ldots \; p_k]$ be any initial p.d. (cf. (0.10)) and let $[p_1^{(n)} \; p_2^{(n)} \ldots \; p_k^{(n)}]$ be the corresponding p.d. at step n ; of course:

$$p_i^{(n)} = \Sigma_j \, p_j \, p_{ji}^{(n)} . \tag{0.27}$$

Now letting n go to the infinity, by (0.21) - we have from (0.27):

$$\lim_{n \to \infty} p_i^{(n)} = w_i \qquad (1 < i < k)$$

stated in words: regardless of what the initial p.d. may be, as n goes to the infinity, the p.d. on the states tends to the stationary p.d.

From theorems (0.5) and (0.6) we can also conclude that: an irreducible aperiodic chain has an invariant p.d. $\{w_j\}$ iff the chain is ergodic; in this case $w_j > 0$ for all j.

If the chain is reducible the following theorem is true:

Theorem 0.7 - If a Markov chain possesses an invariant p.d. $\{w_i\}$, then $w_i = 0$ for every transient or null state s_i.

In other words: the probability of finding the process in the set of ergodic states tends to 1 as n increases.

The following theorem is very important, also Because it yields a general criterion for testing the existence of a stationary p.d.

Theorem 0.8 - The finite chain characterized by the stochastic matrix Π has a stationary p.d. iff there exists an integer N such that Π^N has a positive column.

Remark that this condition can be expressed equivalently by saying that there should be a state reachable in N steps from any state of the chain.

Of course the condition is fulfilled if Π^N is a positive matrix for some N (in particular if Π is a positive matrix) and moreover:

Theorem 0.9 - If Π^N is positive for some N, then all the elements of the stationary p.d. are positive.

It is important to investigate about the rapidity of the convergence of $p_{ij}^{(n)}$ towards w_j, in case the stationary p.d. exists. To this end, let

$$(0.28) \qquad M_j^{(n)} = \max_{1 \leq i \leq k} p_{ij}^{(n)}$$

$$(1 \leq j \leq k)$$

$$(0.29) \qquad m_j^{(n)} = \min_{1 \leq i \leq k} p_{ij}^{(n)}$$

be the greatest and the smallest element respectively of the j-th column of Π^n. Then the following statements are true:

the sequence (0.28) of the max is nonincreasing with n
the sequence (0.29) of the min is nondecreasing with n
therefore the sequence

$$d_j^{(n)} \overset{\text{def}}{=} M_j^{(n)} - m_j^{(n)} \tag{0.30}$$

is nonincreasing with n , and moreover since

$$0 \leqslant m_j^{(n)} \leqslant M_j^{(n)} \leqslant 1 \tag{0.31}$$

also

$$0 \leqslant d_j^{(n)} \leqslant 1$$

for every n .

The following theorem is true

Theorem 0.10 - The following limits exist:

$$\lim_{n\to\infty} M_j^{(n)} \quad ; \quad \lim_{n\to\infty} m_j^{(n)} \quad ; \quad \lim_{n\to\infty} d_j^{(n)}$$

and moreover

$$\lim_{n\to\infty} M_j^{(n)} = \lim_{n\to\infty} m_j^{(n)} \tag{0.32}$$

$$\lim_{n\to\infty} d_j^{(n)} = 0 \tag{0.33}$$

On the other hand, since by (0.28) and (0.29)

$$m_j^{(n)} \leqslant p_{ij}^{(n)} \leqslant M_j^{(n)} \tag{0.34}$$

and since by assumption $p_{ij}^{(n)}$ tends towards w_j, by (0.32) we see that the sequence of the $M_j^{(n)}$ tends to w_j from above and the sequence of the $m_j^{(n)}$ tends to w_j from below:

Theorem 0.11 - The limiting behaviour of the sequences $M_j^{(n)}$ and $m_j^{(n)}$ as n goes to ∞ is as follows:

$$M_j^{(n)} \downarrow w_j \;;\; m_j^{(n)} \uparrow w_j \qquad (1 \leq j \leq k) \tag{0.35}$$

As to the speed of convergence of $p_{ij}^{(n)}$ towards w_j the following theorem gives us an answer:

Theorem 0.12 - For every value of n we have

$$p_{ij}^{(n)} = w_j + b_{ij}^{(n)} \tag{0.36}$$

where

$$\left| b_{ij}^{(n)} \right| \leq \beta \tau^n \tag{0.37}$$

being β a positive number and being

$$0 < \tau < 1. \tag{0.38}$$

Theorem 0.12 expresses a kind of exponential speed of convergence of the elements of Π^n towards the elements of the stationary p.d.

Chapter 1

THE TRANSMISSION LINK AND SOURCE CODING PROBLEM

1.1. The block diagram for the communication link.

In this chapter we want to provide an informal review of some fundamental concepts concerning the different parts which make up a Communication Link. The discussion is not intended to be rigorous or complete; its aim, rather, is to give a rough survey of the items covered.

In what follows we shall refer to a Communication Link as schematized in the following picture

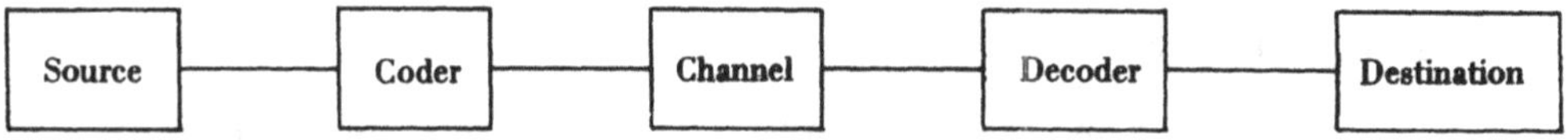

Fig. 1.1. Block Diagram for the Communication Link

In spite of its oversimplified character, if compared with most actual communication chains, this scheme proves to be extremely useful and many of the results obtained for it can be help for studying actual systems.

One peculiar characteristic of this diagram is that it represents the system as cut in its main constituent parts (the Source, the Coder, etc.), and this permits, al least to some extent, as we shall see, to study each part without referring to the others. Each block is analysed as a mathematical entity, and the composition of the different parts into one unity is a further mathematical problem. This " matching" problem is by no means solved when the problems relative to the single parts of the link have been solved.

Although challenging and interesting in its own, this mathematical analysis could perhaps result in a useless job if it had no contact with the practical implementation and with the real problems of actual transmission systems. Actually, these practical considerations play an important role in the choice of the mathematical models contained in the different blocks of the diagram of fig. 1.1 or in the interpretation of the properties resulting form this analysis. Here the theory impacts strongly on the reality.

An important remark is that the five blocks in fig. 1.1 are not homogeneous, i.e. - as it happens in many situations of interest - the Source, the Channel and the Destination, are to be considered as given once and for all, without any possibility of changing their characteristic parameters out of very narrow ranges, while on the other hand the Coder and the Decoder have a much greater flexibility.

More than that, Coder and Decoder are specifically designed by the communication engineer, who by means of these two blocks, tries to cope with the fundamental problem of faithfully transmitting the information output by the Source to the Destination, through the Channel.

It is apparent that a greater number of Coder-Decoder pairs could be designed, at least in principle, for a given Source - Channel - Destination triplet and that an optimal choice should be made among these pairs, taking into account as many parameters as necessary (e.g. cost, reliability, faithfulness, etc.). But in practice, the family Coder-Decoder pairs is strongly limited by essential mathematical difficulties; naturally, mathematical tractability can be included among the design parameters, thus bringing to an "optimal" choice within a much more restricted class of Coder-Decoder pairs.

1.2. Necessity of coder and decoder.

It should be kept in mind that no Destination wishes to receive information with an infinite degree of accuracy, and this for many practical reasons (storage problems, time difficulties, etc.). Therefore it is sufficient to transmit the Source output the Channel with a finite degree of accuracy.

In general the output of the Source has a form that cannot be accepted by the Channel (e.g. for physical reasons), while the output of the Channel cannot be accepted by the Destination. This "mismatch" between Source-Destination and Channel should be removed by a translation from the Source alphabet into the Channel alphabet and viceversa. This translation introduces in most cases a certain information loss, which should be kept under a certain level, depending on the accuracy requirements imposed by the Destination. Thus the first major reason for the introduction of the Coder-Decoder pair becomes apparent: it should provide the Channel with an "understandable" and sufficiently accurate representation of the information generated by the Source. After transmission through the Channel and processing through the Decoder, the Destination should be able, in its turn, to go back to the information output by the Source, within the accuracy level agreed upon beforehand.

Once the matching between Source-Destination and Channel is granted, there is still another danger for the transmission accuracy, i.e. the transmission errors, which are unavoidable in every real transmission link, and stem from many different causes, collectively called "noise". Information should be protected against these errors, and this constitutes the second major task for the Coder-Decoder pair.

It can be shown that if the protection against the transmission errors is good enough, the information loss between Source output and Destination input reduces to the (possible) information loss introduced during the translation performed by the Coder.

It is one of the most brilliant results of Information Theory that there exists a "universal" form for the information produced by a very broad class of Sources (in other words the output of these Sources can be translated into this form with an accuracy level whatsoever); and even more: this universal form - which is a sequence of binary digits - is universal also for a large class of transmission Channel (stated differently: a binary sequence can be translated into a sequence of letters taken from the Channel alphabet). This pivotal theorem permits to break the translation-and-representation task of the Coder-Decoder pair into two distinct and independent steps. The first step consists in translating the Source output into a binary sequence, whose rate (in binary digits/sec) should be sufficiently high as to grant the desired level of accuracy. The second step consists in translating the resulting binary sequence into a Channel sequence whose rate (in Channel digits/sec) is uniquely determined by the Channel alphabet size and by the rate of the binary sequence.

This separation of the translation into two steps suggests in a natural way the idea of splitting Coder and Decoder into two separate blocks each, to be called Source Coder (and Source Decoder) and Channel Coder (and Decoder) whose task should be clear from the previous discussion. Of course the Channel Coder can also be given the task of protecting the encoded information against the transmission errors, and this without interferring with the representation task of the Source Coder. Correspondingly the Channel Decoder performs also a kind of inverse information processing, aiming at elim inating any protecting superstructure from the Channel output.

The splitting of Coder and Decoder we have been illustrating leads to the following block diagram for the information transmission link:

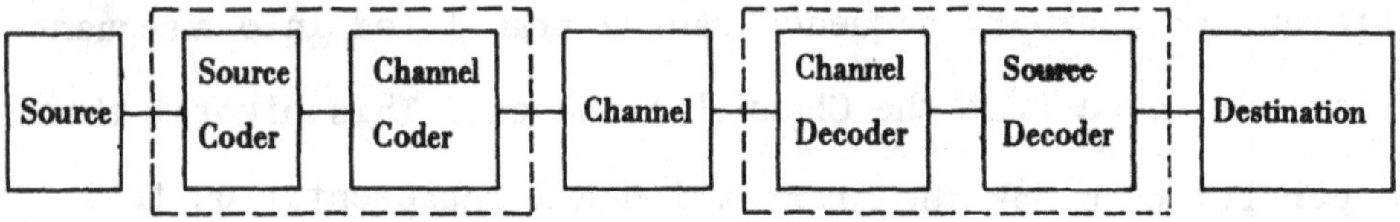

Fig. 1.2. Separating Coder and Decoder into Two Distinct Blocks.

We wish to emphasize that the possibility of splitting Coder and Decoder into two separate parts and the huge simplification resulting in the design of the transmission link are not as trivial as it could appear at a first glance. Actually this possibility strongly rests upon the existence of the universal form for information we have mentioned before.

1.3. Source rate and channel capacity.

The blocks of fig. 2 could also be grouped together differently, to give rise to a "binary transmission link", as depicted in fig. 1.3

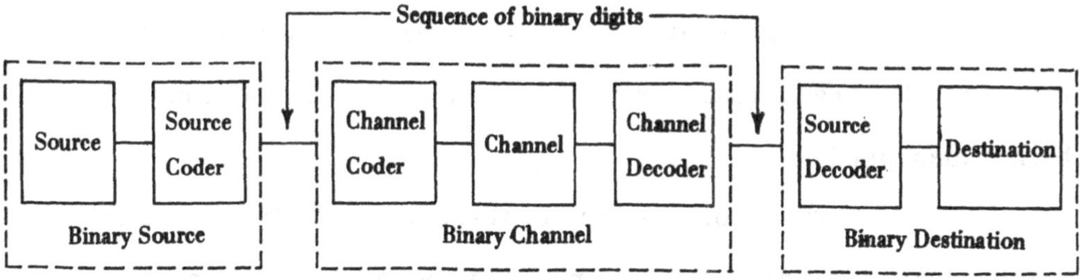

Fig. 1.3. The Binary Transmission Link.

According to the block diagram of fig. 1.3, the output of the binary Source represents, up to a given accuracy level (see next number for more details), the output of the original Source, by means of a sequence of binary digits. This sequence has a certain rate (in bits/sec or in bits/binary digit) which cannot be lower than a given amount if the accuracy requirements in the Source representation are to be met. The binary sequence is thereafter fed into a Binary Channel, whence a (possibly different) binary sequence comes out.

Here a general property of transmission Channels comes in, namely Channel capacity. The capacity of a Channel can be defined - in an informal way - as the greatest rate (in bits/sec, or in bits/Channel symbol) at which information can be sent errorless over the Channel. Of course the absence of errors is obtained by proper coding and decoding methods, and by introducing a certain transmission delay; but what matters is that it is only necessary to slow down the information rate just under the Channel capacity for getting errorless transmission. Conversely, however, if the rate is greater than the capacity, it is not possible to get an arbitrarily small probability for the transmission errors, regardless of the encoding techniques used.

Therefore we are confronted with two partially independent requirements: on one hand we must represent the Source output with a certain accuracy, and therefore the information rate of the binary digits entering the Channel should not be smaller than a given amount, R say; on the other hand transmission errors should be avoided, and therefore the information rate of the same sequence of binary digits must not exceed the Channel capacity, C say. As a consequence, a solution for the problem of transmitting errorless within the given range exists if, and only if, R does not exceed C . If this condition is met, then the only information loss between the original Source output and the original Destination input is, possibly, to be found between the ends of the Source Coder, which performs the conversion of the Source output into the binary sequence; this information loss is - by the very "construction" of the process - completely tolerable.

Of course there exist cases in which the conversion into the binary alphabet operated by the Source Coder does not bring in any information loss. This may happen when the original Source is discrete.

1.4. Discrete and continuous sources.

What we have said so far applies in general to every kind of information Sources (or rather to every kind of mathematical model of an information Source). It is advisable, however, to point out that a very important distinction can be made between discrete Source and Continuous (or "Waveform") Sources.

A discrete Source is a Source whose output is a sequence of random variables:

$$\ldots\ldots X_{-1}\, X_0\, X_1 \ldots\ldots$$

Each of this random variables can take on a finite number of values, which may be assumed to be the same for all of the variables. Let

$$\mathcal{A} = \left\{ a_1, a_2, \ldots, a_k \right\}$$

be the set of these values, or letters; $\mathcal{A}$ is called the "Source alphabet". Each of the above-mentioned random variables takes a value in $\mathcal{A}$ according to a conditional probability distribution which in general depends on the previous letters output by the Source (this is expressed by saying that the Source has "memory'; if there is no such dependence the Source is said to be "memoryless").

Referring now to the previous discussion, it is easy to see that if we wish to encode the Source output by means of a binary alphabet, it is sufficient (but not necessary in general) to use K binary words od length $\lceil \log K \rceil$* to provide a lossless binary representation of the Source. Actually something more can be achieved, but for the moment we content ourselves with the above observation, which can be restated as follows:

it is always possible to give a lossless binary representation of a Discrete Source.

As to Continuous Sources, the situation is quite different. From a mathematical point of view, a Continuous Source is a random process, whose realizations are continuous real functions of a real variable (time).

It is therefore apparent that it is not possible to encode the output of a Continuous Source by means of a binary (or, more generally finite) alphabet, unless we are ready to tolerate a certain "distortion" between the original waveform and the waveform that can be reconstructed starting from the coded discrete sequence. If we wish to assess this distortion, it is necessary to introduce a "distance" between waveforms; on the basis of this distance function, an equivalence relationship between waveforms is defined: two waveforms are said to be equivalent if their distance is not greater than

(*) $\lceil x \rceil$ denotes the smallest integer $\geq x$; $\lfloor x \rfloor$ denotes the greatest integer $\leq x$; logarithms are always taken to the base 2, unless differently stated.

a given value, which depends on the greatest tolerated distortion. This equivalence relationship, together with additional considerations, concerning e.g. the transmission power, essentially reduces the Continuous Source to a Discrete Source.

The price we must pay for getting a Discrete Source out of a Continuous one is some information loss in this "analog-to-digital" transformation. On the other hand this information loss can be made as small as we like simply by enlarging the size of the resulting Discrete Source alphabet. At this point, the output of the resulting Discrete Source can be encoded without any additional information loss.

We can assume that the analog-to-digital reduction is accomplished by a device called "equivalence classifier", which is fed by the Source and whose output is a sequence of letters from the resulting Discrete Source alphabet (these letters can be considered as "representative waveforms" for the different equivalence classes). In this way we arrive at a Discrete Source (see fig. 1.4) which is equivalent to the original Continuous Source, up to the Distortion introduced by the equivalence classifier.

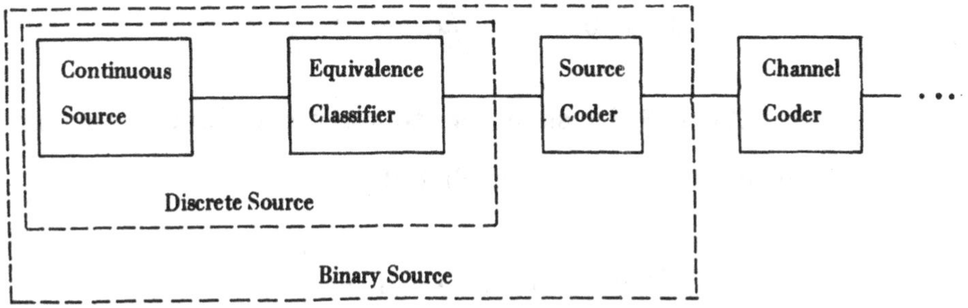

Fig. 1.4. The Discrete Source generated by the Equivalence Classifier.

As we have already pointed out, if we wish to decrease the amount of average distortion, we increase the size of the alphabet of the Discrete Source; this amounts in its turn to increasing the rate of the resulting Binary Source (see fig. 1.4)

In the sequel we shall focus our attention on Discrete Sources.

Chapter 2

CODING FOR DISCRETE MEMORYLESS SOURCES

2.1. The problem posed.

We shall consider a Discrete Memoryless Source (DMS), which can be represented by a finite scheme:

$$\mathcal{S} = \begin{pmatrix} a_1 & a_2 & \dots & a_k \\ p_1 & p_2 & \dots & p_k \end{pmatrix} \tag{2.1}$$

with the usual conditions

$$p_i > 0 \qquad \sum_1^k {}_i \, p_i = 1 \tag{2.2}$$

The DMS is supposed to emit one letter each unit of time, choosing it from its alphabet

$$\mathcal{A} = \left\{ a_1, a_2, \dots, a_k \right\} \tag{2.3}$$

according to the probability distribution (p.d.)

$$\mathcal{P} = \left\{ p_1 \ p_2 \ \dots \ p_k \right\}. \tag{2.4}$$

As a consequence, the probability of a sequence $\underline{u}^L$ of length L, say

$$\underline{u}^{(L)} = u_1 \, u_2 \dots u_L \qquad u_i \in \mathcal{A} \tag{2.5}$$

is given by the product of the probabilities of its various letters:

$$\text{Prob}\left(\underline{u}^{(L)}\right) = \text{Prob}(u_1)\,\text{Prob}(u_2)\dots\text{Prob}(u_L). \tag{2.6}$$

Along with the Source alphabet $\mathcal{A}$ given in (2.3) we shall consider a Channel alphabet $\mathcal{C}$, of size D. The Coder transforms sequences of letters from $\mathcal{A}$ into sequences of letters from $\mathcal{C}$. In many practical instances the transmission cost is proportional to the length of the encoded sequences which we shall label by $\underline{s}^{(N)}$ if N is its length:

$$\underline{s}^{(N)} = s_1 \ s_2 \dots s_N \qquad \left(s_i \in \mathcal{C}\right) \tag{2.7}$$

An encoded sequence like that in (2.7) will be called a 'codeword" of length N.

Now the task of the Coder (*) can be described

(*) Apart from the information processing for securing protection against transmission errors, which is neglected here.

as follows: the original Source sequence $u_1 u_2 \ldots$ is splitted into a sequence of subsequences, each of length L , as the one in (2.5), and therefore one can think of the Source as emitting a sequence of the following form:

$$\underline{u}_1^{(L)} \, \underline{u}_2^{(L)} \ldots \tag{2.8}$$

Subsequently to each of the sequences $\underline{u}_i^{(L)}$ the Coder associates a codeword $\underline{s}_i^{(N_i)} = \Phi(\underline{u}_i^{(L)})$, whose length N_i depends in general on the Source sequence $u_i^{(L)}$:

$$N_i = N_i(u_i^{(L)}). \tag{2.9}$$

Therefore, when the Coder is fed with the sequence (2.8), it outputs a sequence

$$\Phi(\underline{u}_1^{(L)})\,\Phi(\underline{u}_2^{(L)}) \ldots\ldots = \underline{s}_1^{(N_1)} \, \underline{s}_2^{(N_2)} \ldots \tag{2.10}$$

Φ is the "code mapping", which defines the rule by which a codeword is associated to a Source sequence.

If we wish to decrease the transmission cost, we should decrease the average length of the codewords, which can be done, roughly, by choosing such a Φ which associates probable Source sequences with short codewords and unprobable Source sequences with long codewords, while respecting some specific rules for granting unique decipherability (such as the prefix property and the like). There is a set of techniques used for decreasing the average length of the codewords known as "variable-length coding techniques". We do not intend to enter into details, we only wish to point out that these techniques suffer from a serious disadvantage, which consists, loosely speaking, in the necessity of introducing between Coder and Channel a Buffer of infinite capacity. This fact urges us to adopt a quite different strategy, i.e. to use the so called "fixed-length encoding techniques".

In this case the situation is as follows: we wish to encode sequences of length L made up with letters taken from the alphabet $\mathcal{A}$ of size K into codewords of length N made up with letters taken from the alphabet $\mathcal{C}$ of size D.

Since there are K^L different Source sequences and D^N different codewords, if we wish the code function Φ to have an inverse, then N should satisfy

$$D^N \geqslant K^L \tag{2.11}$$

or equivalently

$$N \geqslant L \frac{\log K}{\log D} \tag{2.12}$$

Eq. (2.12) sets a lower bound on the codeword length, and if it is satisfied, a one-one correspondence between Source sequences and codewords is granted, which makes it possible (if transmission errors have no effect) to recover the information emitted by the Source with zero error probability. Seen from this viewpoint, fixed length techniques are not very attractive, since the lower bound of eq. (2.12) is rather poor. Actually much more can be done: it is possible to substantially decrease the lower bound on N , while keeping the error probability, P_e , arbitrarily close to zero. The price one must pay for this decrease in the lower bound on N is a delay in the transmission process: actually, for making P_e go to zero, it is necessary to increase L , and since the first codeword is sent through the Channel $L\sigma$ seconds after (*) the Source started transmitting ($1/\sigma$ is the Source rate in symbol/sec), it is clear that the transmission delay increases when P_e is made decrease.

2.2. Shannon theorem for source coding.

We have seen that if we insist on adopting fixed-length encoding and we want to lower the codeword length below the bound expressed by (2.12), we must give up the one-one correspondence between Source sequences and codewords. Stated differently, if W is the number of distinct codewords and

$$W < K^{L} \tag{2.13}$$

(*) We assume that the Coder introduces no delay in transforming the input sequence into the corresponding codeword.

then there exist codewords to which more than one Source sequence are associated. One is led to associate distinct codewords to the W most probable Source sequences, while encoding arbitrarily the remaining $K^L - W$. The decoding rule should then be as follows: on reception of a codeword, it has to be decoded in the most probable of the sequences from which it can derive. Then a decoding error occurs if, and only if, the Source emits one of the $K^L - W$ least probable sequences. Therefore the overall error probability, P_e, coincides with the sum of the probabilities of those sequences.

Let $\mathcal{B}_L^{(W)}$ be the set of the most probable L-length Source sequences, and let $\bar{\mathcal{B}}_L^{(W)}$ be its complementary set; then

$$P_e = \text{Prob}\left(\bar{\mathcal{B}}_L^{(W)}\right) = \sum_{\underline{u}^L \in \bar{\mathcal{B}}_L^W} \text{Prob}\left(\underline{u}^{(L)}\right) \qquad (2.14)$$

So far we are not sure that there exists a solution for our problem of encoding the L-sequences in such way that:

1) the error probability P_e is kept under a prescribed level;
2) there is a substantial reduction in the uniform length of the codewords with respect to the trivial bound of eq. (2.12).

An answer in the positive is provided by the following theorem of Shannon:

<u>Theorem 2.1</u> Let it be given a DMS with entropy H (*) generating sequences of length L from an alphabet $\mathcal{A}$ of size K. Then if

$$N \geqslant L \frac{H+\delta}{\log D} \tag{2.15}$$

it is possible to encode these sequences into codewords of length N of symbols taken from an alphabet $\mathcal{C}$ of size D in such a way that for any $\varepsilon > 0$ the probability of erroneous decoding P_e satisfies

$$P_e < 0$$

provided L is large enough, whatever the positive constant δ is.

Conversely, no matter what the encoding procedure is, if

$$N \leqslant L \frac{H-\delta}{\log D} \tag{2.16}$$

then

$$P_e > 1 - \varepsilon$$

(*) The entropy of a DMS is given by $H = -\sum_{1}^{k} {}_{i}\, p_i \log p_i$ (cf. (2.4)).

for arbitrary $\varepsilon > 0$, provided L is large enough, whatever the positive δ is.

Remark. The gist of this theorem lies in the comparison between the Source entropy H and the quantity

$$R = \frac{N \log D}{L} \tag{2.17}$$

which is called the "encoding rate". Of course D^N coincides with the number W of different codewords (cf. (2.13).).

Proof. Define the self-information of the event x having probability $p(x)$ as the quantity

$$I(x) = - \log p(x) \tag{2.18}$$

By (2.6) and (2.18) the self-information of the sequence $\underline{u}$ is given by

$$\begin{aligned} I(\underline{u}^{(L)}) = - \log \mathrm{Prob}(\underline{u}^{(L)}) = \sum_1^L{}_i \left\{ - \log \mathrm{Prob}(u_i) \right\} = \\ \sum_1^k{}_i \; I(u_i) \end{aligned} \tag{2.19}$$

where $I(u_i) = -\log \mathrm{Prob}\,(u_i)$ is the self-information of the i-th letter. The letters in $\underline{u}^{(L)}$ are identically distributed independent r.v.s , and by (2.18) self-information is a one-one function of probability; it follows that the weak law of large numbers applies: for any $\delta > 0$ there exists an $\varepsilon(L, \delta)$ such that

(2.20) $$\text{Prob}\left\{ \underline{u}^{(L)} : \left| \frac{I(\underline{u}^{(L)})}{L} - H \right| > \delta \right\} \leqslant \varepsilon(L,\delta)$$

and

$$\lim_{L\to\infty} \varepsilon(L,\delta) = 0$$

We emphasize that H is the mean value of the r.v. $I(u)$ which takes on the value $-\log p_i$ with probability p_i.

Let us call "(L,δ)-typical seuqences" those $\underline{u}^{(L)}$ for which

(2.21) $$\left| \frac{I(u^{(L)})}{L} - H \right| < \delta$$

and let $\mathcal{T}_{L,\delta}$ be the set of the (L,δ)-typical sequences. Then by (2.20):

(2.22) $$\text{Prob}\,(\mathcal{T}_{L,\delta}) \geqslant 1 - \varepsilon(L,\delta)$$

and moreover

(2.23) $$L(H-\delta) \leqslant I(\underline{u}^{(L)}) \leqslant L(H+\delta)$$

or equivalently

(2.24) $$2^{-L(H-\delta)} \geqslant p(\underline{u}^{(L)})\ 2^{-L(H+\delta)}$$

whenever $\underline{u}^{(L)}$ belongs to $\mathcal{T}_{L,\delta}$.

We can also give a precise evaluation for the

number $M_{L,\delta}$ of sequences in $\mathcal{T}_{L,\delta}$. By (2.24) we have

$$1 \geq \text{Prob}(\mathcal{T}_{L,\delta}) \geq M_{L,\delta} \cdot \min_{\underline{u}^{(L)} \in \mathcal{T}_{L,\delta}} \text{Prob}(\underline{u}^{(L)}) \geq M_{L,\delta} 2^{-L(H+\delta)}$$

whence

$$M_{L,\delta} \leq 2^{L(H+\delta)} \tag{2.25}$$

On the other hand, still by (2.24) we have

$$1 - \varepsilon(L,\delta) \leq P(\mathcal{T}_{L,\delta}) \leq M_{L,\delta} \cdot \max_{\underline{u}^{(L)} \in \mathcal{T}_{L,\delta}} \text{Prob}(\underline{u}^{(L)}) \leq M_{L,\delta} 2^{-L(H-\delta)}$$

whence

$$M_{L,\delta} \geq \left\{1 - \varepsilon(L,\delta)\right\} 2^{L(H-\delta)} \tag{2.26}$$

which gives, together with (2.25), the desired evaluation for $M_{L,\delta}$.

The situation is as follows: the (L,δ)-typical sequences, which are approximately 2^{LH} have an overall probability which is as close to 1 as wish (cf. (2.22)). Since

$$\lim_{L \to \infty} \frac{2^{LH}}{K^L} = 0 \tag{2.27}$$

if $H < \log K$ (i.e. if the probability distribution (2.4) is not the uniform one), the typical sequences are "very few" if compared with all the sequences; but if we provide distinct codewords for the typical sequences, the probability of erroneous decoding is upper bounded by $\varepsilon(L,\delta)$

The (L, δ)-typical sequences are therefore sufficient to represent the Source adequately, up to $\varepsilon(L, \delta)$

Now, if N satisfies inequality (2.15), then

$$D^N \geqslant M_{L,\delta}$$

and the first part of the theorem is proved (remark that when L is increased to make P_e less than any positive quantity, N should also be increased, to make (2.15) be satisfied).

To prove the second part of the theorem, rewrite eq. (2.16) as follows

$$N \leqslant \frac{H - 2\delta}{\log_2 D} \tag{2.28}$$

which does not destroy generality. If N satisfies (2.28) the codewords are at most $2^{L(H-2\delta)}$. If we associate an (L, δ)-typical sequence to each codeword, the overall probability of the encoded typical sequences does not exceed $2^{-L(H-\delta)} \cdot 2^{L(H-2\delta)} = 2^{-L\delta}$. One could however feel it appropriate to choose a different strategy; i.e. one could let some typical sequence without codeword while encoding some non-typical very probable sequences. The overall probability of the non-typical sequences does not exceed $\varepsilon(L, \delta)$, and consequently the total probability of the L-sequences for which we provide codewords is upperbounded by

$$\varepsilon(L, \delta) + 2^{-L\delta}$$

whence the conclusion that P_e tends to 1 as L goes to the infinity, for any $\delta > 0$. Q.d.e.

We wish to point out that assigning distinct codewords to the typical sequences is completely equivalent to assigning distinct codewords to a convenient number of the most probable L -sequences. Taking into account the definition (2.17) of the encoding rate R, we can state the following theorem whose simple proof is omitted for brevity's sake:

Theorem 2.2 If distinct codewords are provided for the most probable 2^{RL}-sequences, then

$$\begin{cases} \text{if } R > H & P \downarrow 0 \\ & \qquad \text{as } L \to \infty \\ \text{if } R < H & P \uparrow 1 \end{cases}$$

2.3. Testing a simple alternative hypothesis

Although very important, the result expressed by Theorems 2.1 and 2.2 tells us nothing about the speed at which P_e goes to zero as L increases, when R is greater than H. Actually the asymptotic behaviour of P_e is extremely important; the complexity of encoding and decoding apparatus grows with L, and therefore an exacte estimate of the L needed for achieving a desired error probability is very useful. We wish now to give a certain number of theorems from Statistics, which are very useful for our purposes. It is necessary to introduce briefly the Testing of a Simple Alternative Hypothesis. For simplicity's sake we shall restrict to the finite case.

Consider a finite set Ω and the set $\mathcal{P}(\Omega)$ of the subsets of Ω; assume that one of two probability distributions μ_1 and μ_2 has been assigned to the probability space $(\Omega, \mathcal{P}(\Omega))$, but we do not know which one. To guess the distribution actually present in the space, we choose a point x in Ω according to the unknown p.d. We divide Ω into two disjoint subsets E_1 and E_2 :

(2.29) $$E_1 \cup E_2 = \Omega \quad ; \quad E_1 \cap E_2 = \emptyset$$

and adopt the following decision rule:

1) if $x \in E_1$ we say that μ_1 is true and reject μ_2

2) if $x \in E_2$ we say that μ_2 is true and reject μ_1.

This strategy may lead to two kinds of errors, namely:

i) μ_2 is the true distribution and yet x belongs to E_1 (which causes us to state wrongly that μ_1 is true); this mistake is the "error of the first kind" and has a probability given by

(2.30) $$\mu_2(E_1) \triangleq \gamma$$

ii) μ_1 is the true distribution and x belongs to E_2 (which causes us to state wrongly that μ_2 is true); this is the "error of the second kind" and has a probability given by

$$\mu_1(E_2) \triangleq \beta . \tag{2.31}$$

To improve our guess, we can also choose n subsequent independent samples $x_1, x_2, \ldots, x_n$ from Ω, or equivalently one sample from Ω^n. The decision then depends on whether $x^{(n)} = (x_1, \ldots, x_n)$ belongs to $E_1^{(n)}$ or to $E_2^{(n)}$, with

$$E_1^{(n)} \cup E_2^{(n)} = \Omega^n \; ; \quad E_1^{(n)} \cap E_2^{(n)} = \emptyset$$

The choice of $E_1^{(n)}$ and $E_2^{(n)}$ is important in the following problem: for any fixed value γ_0 ($0 < \gamma_0 < 1$) of the error of the first kind, minimize the error of the second kind, i.e. find the quantity:

$$\beta_n^* \triangleq \inf_{E_1^{(n)} :\; \mu_2(E_1^{(n)}) = \gamma_0} \mu_1(E_2^{(n)}) \tag{2.32}$$

or conversely, for any fixed value $\beta_0 (0 < \beta_0 < 1)$ of the error of the second kind, minimize the error of the first kind, i.e. find the quantity

$$\gamma_n^* \triangleq \inf_{E_2^{(n)} :\; \mu_1(E_2^{(n)}) = \beta_0} \mu_2(E_1^{(n)}) \tag{2.33}$$

We are interested in the asymptotic behaviour (as n goes to ∞) of the infima β_n^* and γ_n^*, and one helpful tool in this respect is the I-divergence (or "informational gain") between μ_1 and μ_2 which is defined as

(2.34) $$I(\mu_1 \| \mu_2) = \sum_1^k{}_i \; \mu_{i1} \log \frac{\mu_{i1}}{\mu_{i2}}$$

being K the number of elements in Ω and μ_{i1}, μ_{i2} the μ_1-and μ_2 -probability of the i -th element in Ω . It is well known that the I -divergence is a nonnegative quantity:

(2.35) $$I(\mu_1 \| \mu_2) \geqslant 0$$

and the equality in (2.35) holds if and only if the two distributions μ_1 and μ_2 coincide; the I -divergence is a non symmetric function of μ_1 and μ_2 .

It is easy to prove the following

Proposition 2.1 If $\mu_i^{(n)}$ $(i = 1, 2)$ is the product distribution of μ_i in Ω , then

(2.36) $$I(\mu_1^{(n)} \| \mu_2^{(n)})^{1)} = n \quad I(\mu_1 \| \mu_2)$$

Now we are in a position to state the following two propositions:

Proposition 2.2 If μ_1 is the true distribution, the samples of length n can be divided into two disjoint sets, $E_1^{(n)}$ and $E_2^{(n)}$. Provided n is large enough, the samples $(x_1, x_2, \ldots, x_n)$. in $E_1^{(n)}$ satisfy the inequality

---

(*) $I(\mu_1^{(n)} \| \mu_2^{(n)})$ is the I-divergence computed on the basis of an n-th sample.

$$\mu_1(x_1)\ \dots\ \mu_1(x_n) \geqslant 2^{n\left[I(\mu_1\|\mu_2)-\varepsilon\right]}\mu_2(x_1)\dots\mu_2(x_n) \tag{2.37}$$

while the samples in $E_2^{(n)}$ occur with probability less than η, being ε and η arbitrary positive numbers.

Proof; This proposition is a direct consequence of the weak law of large numbers. Actually if μ_1 is true, the quantity

$$\frac{1}{n}\log\frac{\mu_1(x_1)\ \dots\ \mu_1(x_n)}{\mu_2(x_1)\ \dots\ \mu_2(x_n)} = \frac{1}{n}\sum_1^n{}_i \log\frac{\mu_1(x_i)}{\mu_2(x_i)} \tag{2.38}$$

tends in probability towards the μ_1-mean value of $\log\dfrac{\mu_1(x)}{\mu_2(x)}$, i.e. towards $I(\mu_1\|\mu_2)$ whence the thesis.

Proposition 2.3 If μ_1 is the true distribution, the samples of length n can be divided into two disjoints sets $E_1^{(n)}$ and $E_2^{(n)}$. Provided n is large enough, the samples $(x_1, x_2, \dots x_n)$ in $E_1^{(n)}$ satisfy the inequality

$$\mu_1(x_1)\ \dots\ \mu_1(x_n) \leqslant 2^{n\left[I(\mu_1\|\mu_2)+\varepsilon\right]}\mu_2(x_1)\dots\mu_2(x_n)$$

while the samples in $E_2^{(n)}$ occur with probability less than δ, being ε and δ arbitrary positive numbers.

Proof; The proof is the same as that of Proposition 2.2

Now, by integrating both sides of (2.37) over the set $E_1^{(n)}$, we get

$$1 \geqslant \mu_1^{(n)}(E_1^{(n)}) \geqslant 2^{n\left[I(\mu_1\|\mu_2)-\varepsilon\right]}\mu_2^{(n)}(E_1^{(n)}) \tag{2.39}$$

whence for any fixed value $\beta_0 (0 < \beta_0 < 1)$ of $\beta = \mu_1^{(n)}(E_2^{(n)})$ or equivalently for $\mu_1^{(n)}(E_1^{(n)}) = 1 - \beta_0$, taking logarithms in eq. (2.39), we get

$$0 \geqslant \log(1-\beta_0) \geqslant n\left[I(\mu_1\|\mu_2) - \varepsilon\right] + \log \mu_2^{(n)}(E_1^{(n)}) \tag{2.40}$$

Dividing by n and passing to the limit as n goes to ∞ we have

$$\lim_{n\to\infty} \frac{1}{n} \log \frac{1}{\mu_2^{(n)}(E^{(n)})} \geqslant I(\mu_1\|\mu_2) - \varepsilon \tag{2.41}$$

In particular, eq (2.41) holds for γ_n^* instead of $\mu_2^{(n)}(E_1^{(n)})$ (cf. definition (2.33)):

$$\lim_{n\to\infty} \frac{1}{n} \log \frac{1}{\gamma_n^*} \geqslant I(\mu_1\|\mu_2) - \varepsilon \tag{2.42}$$

Starting from equation (2.42) the following theorem can be proved:

Theorem 2.3 For any fixed value $\beta_0 (0 < \beta_0 < 1$ of β, we have

$$\lim_{n\to\infty} \frac{1}{n} \log \frac{1}{\gamma_n^*} = I(\mu_1\|\mu_2) \tag{2.43}$$

or equivalently

$$\lim_{n\to\infty} (\gamma_n^*)^{\frac{1}{n}} = 2^{-I(\mu_1\|\mu_2)} \tag{2.44}$$

Proof. Let $E_3^{(n)}$ be the subset of Ω^n defined by

$$2^{n\left[I(\mu_1\|\mu_2)-\varepsilon\right]} \leq \frac{\mu_1(x_1)\dots\mu_1(x_n)}{\mu_2(x_1)\dots\mu_2(x_n)} \, 2^{n\left[I(\mu_1\|\mu_2)+\varepsilon\right]} \tag{2.45}$$

After an integration over $E_3^{(n)}$ from the right inequality we get

$$\mu_1^{(n)}(E_3^{(n)}) < 2^{n\left[I(\mu_1\|\mu_2)+\varepsilon\right]} \cdot \mu_2^{(n)}(E_3^{(n)}) \tag{2.46}$$

On the other hand, by Proposition 2.2 and 2.3, if n is large enough

$$\mu_1^{(n)}(E_3^{(n)}) \geq 1 - \eta - \delta \tag{2.47}$$

and since by definition, $E_3^{(n)}$ is contained in the set $E_1^{(n)}$ of Proposition 2.3, also

$$\mu_2^{(n)}(E_3^{(n)}) < \mu_2^{(n)}(E_1^{(n)}) \tag{2.48}$$

whence by (2.46) and (2.47):

$$1 - \eta - \delta < 2^{n\left[I(\mu_1\|\mu_2)+\varepsilon\right]} \mu_2^{(n)}(E_1^{(n)}). \tag{2.49}$$

Eq. (2.49) holds also when $\delta = \beta_0$ and $\mu_2^{(n)}(E_1^{(n)}) = \gamma_n^*$, in which case it gives

$$1 - \eta - \delta \leq 2^{n\left[I(\mu_1\|\mu_2)+\varepsilon\right]} \gamma_n^* \tag{2.50}$$

Taking logarithms on both sides of eq. (2.50) and letting n go to infinity:

$$\lim_{n\to\infty} \frac{1}{n} \log \frac{1}{\gamma_n^*} \leq I(\mu_1\|\mu_2) + \varepsilon \tag{2.51}$$

which yields the thesis when combined with eq. (2.42).

Q.d.e.

In exactly the same way one can prove the following

<u>Theorem 2.4</u> For any fixed value γ_0 $(0 < \gamma_0 < 1)$ of γ, the limiting behaviour of β_n^* is described by the following expression:

$$\lim_{n\to\infty} \frac{1}{n} \log \frac{1}{\beta_n^*} = I(\mu_2 \| \mu_1) \tag{2.52}$$

or equivalently by

$$\lim_{n\to\infty} (\beta_n^*)^{\frac{1}{n}} = 2^{-I(\mu_2\|\mu_1)} \tag{2.53}$$

Theorems 2.3 and 2.4 provide us with the asymptotic behaviour of β_n^* and γ_n^*, but give no hint as how to choose the sets $E_1^{(n)}$ and $E_2^{(n)}$ in order to achieve the infima β_n^* and γ_n^* of the errors of the second kind and of the first kind. The following theorem, which is a particular case of the Neyman Pearson lemma, is very useful relative to this problem:

<u>Theorem 2.5</u> (Neyman-Pearson lemma). If $E_*^{(n)} \subset \Omega^n$ is a set such that

$$\text{i)}\ \mu_1^{(n)}(E_*^{(n)}) = 1 - \beta_0 \qquad (0 < \beta_0 < 1) \tag{2.54'}$$

$$\text{ii)}\ \underline{v} \notin E_*^{(n)} \text{ implies } \frac{\mu_2(\underline{v})}{\mu_1(\underline{v})} \geq \sup_{\underline{u} \in E_*^{(n)}} \frac{\mu_2(\underline{u})}{\mu_1(\underline{u})} \tag{2.54''}$$

then

$$\gamma_n^* = \mu_2^{(n)}(E_*^{(n)}). \tag{2.55}$$

Proof. Consider any set $E^{(n)} \subset \Omega^{n}$ such that $\mu_1^{(n)}(E^{(n)}) \geq 1 - \beta_0$. We wish to prove that $\mu_2^{(n)}(E^{(n)}) \geq \mu_2^{(n)}(E_*^{(n)})$. Now, since

$$E^{(n)} = (E^{(n)} \cap E_*^{(n)}) \cup (E^{(n)} - E_*^{(n)}) \tag{2.56}$$

$$E_*^{(n)} = (E^{(n)} \cap E_*^{(n)}) \cup (E_*^{(n)} - E^{(n)}) \tag{2.57}$$

the two inequalities

$$\mu_2^{(n)}(E^{(n)}) \geq \mu_1^{(n)}(E^{(n)}) \text{ and } \mu_2(E^{(n)} - E_*^{(n)}) \geq \mu_2(E_*^{(n)} - E^{(n)}) \tag{2.58}$$

are equivalent. So it is sufficient to prove the second of them in order to prove the theorem. To this end consider the following chain of inequalities:

$$\mu_2^{(n)}(E^{(n)} - E_*^{(n)}) = \sum_{\underline{v} \in E^{(n)} - E_*^{(n)}} \mu_2^{(n)}(\underline{v}) = \sum_{\underline{v} \in E^{(n)} - E_*^{(n)}} \frac{\mu_2^{(n)}(\underline{v})}{\mu_1^{(n)}(\underline{v})} \mu_1^{(n)}(\underline{v}) \geq$$

$$\geq \sum_{\underline{v} \in E^{(n)} - E_*^{(n)}} \left[\sup_{\underline{u} \in E_*^{(n)}} \frac{\mu_2^{(n)}(\underline{u})}{\mu_1^{(n)}(\underline{u})} \right] \mu_1^{(n)}(\underline{v}) = \sup_{\underline{u} \in E_*^{(n)}} \frac{\mu_2^{(n)}(\underline{u})}{\mu_1^{(n)}(\underline{u})} \cdot \mu_1^{(n)}(E^{(n)} - E^{(n)}) \overset{\&}{\geq}$$

$$\geq \sup_{\underline{u} \in E_*^{(n)}} \frac{\mu_2^{(n)}(\underline{u})}{\mu_1^{(n)}(\underline{u})} \mu_1^{(n)}(E_*^{(n)} - E^{(n)}) = \sum_{\underline{v} \in E_*^{(n)} - E^{(n)}} \left(\sup_{\underline{u} \in E_*^{(n)}} \frac{\mu_2^{(n)}(\underline{u})}{\mu_1^{(n)}(\underline{u})} \right) \mu_1^{(n)}(\underline{v}) \geq$$

$$\geq \sum_{\underline{v} \in E_*^{(n)} - E^{(n)}} \frac{\mu_2^{(n)}(\underline{v})}{\mu_1^{(n)}(\underline{v})} \mu_1^{(n)}(\underline{v}) = \mu_2^{(n)}(E_*^{(n)} - E^{(n)})$$

being the inequality marked by & a consequence of eq. (2.56) (2.57) and of the assumption $\mu_1^{(n)}(E^{(n)}) \geq 1 - \beta_0 = \mu_1^{(n)}(E_*^{(n)})$. This proves the second inequality in (2.58) and the theorem.

In quite a similar way the following theorem

can be proved:

Theorem 2.6 If $E_{**}^{(n)} \subset \Omega^n$ is a set such that $\mu_2^{(n)}(E_{**}^{(n)}) = 1 - \gamma_0$ and if $\underline{v} \notin E_{**}^{(n)}$ implies $\frac{\mu_1^{(n)}(\underline{v})}{\mu_2^{(n)}(\underline{v})} \geq \sup_{u \in E_{**}^{(n)}} \frac{\mu_1^{(n)}(\underline{u})}{\mu_2^{(n)}(\underline{u})}$ then $\beta_n^* = \mu_1(E_{**}^{(n)})$.

4.2. Application to coding for discrete memoryless sources.

On the basis of the preceding results, it is possible to give an alternative proof of Shannon theorem 2.1. Consider theorem 2.5 and put L instead of n, P instead of β_0, $\mathcal{P} \triangleq \{p_1, p_2, \ldots, p_k\}$ instead of μ_1, $\mathcal{U} \triangleq \left\{\frac{1}{k}, \ldots, \frac{1}{k}\right\}$ instead of μ_2 with the usual meaning of the notations. Then the set $E_*^{(n)}$ of theorem 2.5 becomes a set $E_*^{(L)}$ having the following properties:

(2.59') i) $P(E_*^{(L)}) = 1 - P_e$

(2.59'') ii) $\underline{v} \notin E_*^{(L)}$ implies $\left(\frac{1}{k}\right)^L \frac{1}{p(\underline{v})} \geq \sup_{\underline{u} \in E_*^{(L)}} \left(\frac{1}{k}\right)^L \frac{1}{p(\underline{u})}$

i.e. $p(\underline{v}) \leq \inf_{\underline{u} \in E_*^{(L)}} p(\underline{u})$

where $p(\underline{u})$ is the usual product probability of the L-length sequence $\underline{u}$.

In other words, $E_*^{(L)}$ is the set of the most P probable sequences of length L whose overall probability is $1 - P_e$.

The $\mathcal{U}$-measure of a set $E^{(L)} \subset \Omega$ is proportional to the number $|E^{(L)}|$ of elements in $E^{(L)}$, and therefore finding the minimum of $\mathcal{U}(E^{(L)})$ is equivalent to finding the minimum of $|E^{(L)}|$. The proportionality coefficient is $\left(\frac{1}{k}\right)^L$.

Now eq. (2.55) gives us for $\mu_2 = \mathcal{U}$

$$\gamma_n^* = \mathcal{U}(E_*^{(L)}) = \left(\frac{1}{k}\right)^L \left| E_*^{(L)} \right| \tag{2.60}$$

and since by (2.44) $\gamma_n^* \cong 2^{LI(\mathcal{P}\|\mathcal{U})}$ from (2.60) we have

$$\left| E_*^{(L)} \right| \cong K^L 2^{LI(\mathcal{P}\|\mathcal{U})} \tag{2.61}$$

On the other hand the definition (2.34) of the I -divergence gives us

$$I(\mathcal{P}\|\mathcal{U}) = \sum_1^k{}_i \, p_i \log p_i K = \log K - H \tag{2.62}$$

where $H = -\sum_1^k{}_i \, p_i \log p_i$ is the entropy of the DMS. Substituting (2.62) in (2.61) we get precisely Shannon theorem in the following form:

<u>Theorem 2.7</u> No matter what the value P_e $(0 > P_e > 1)$ of the tolerated probability of erroneous decoding is, it is possible to encode the L -length sequences output by a DMS having entropy H by means of no less than $\sim 2^{LH}$ distinct code words.

Now if we wish to study the asymptotic behaviour of P_e as L goes to ∞ , it is necessary to introduce, along with the original p.d. $\mathcal{P}$ of the DMS, a family of auxiliary p.d.s. on the alphabet $\mathcal{A}$. Actually set for any positive number α :

$$\mathcal{Q}_\alpha = \left\{ q_{\alpha 1}, q_{\alpha 2}, \dots, q_{\alpha k} \right\} \tag{2.63}$$

where

$$q_{\alpha i} = \frac{q_i^{\alpha}}{\sum_{j=1}^{k} q_j^{\alpha}} . \tag{2.64}$$

The function $H(\alpha)$ defined by

$$H(\alpha) = - \sum_{i=1}^{k} q_{\alpha i} \log q_{\alpha i} \qquad (\alpha > 0) \tag{2.65}$$

which is the entropy of the p.d. $\mathcal{Q}_\alpha$, has the following properties:

1) $H(\alpha)$ is a continuous function of α for $\alpha > 0$;
2) $H(\alpha)$ is a strictly decreasing function of α; this is not true if $\mathcal{P}$ is the uniform p.d., in which case $H(\alpha)$ is constant, but this case will always be neglected, since it is trivial;
3) $\lim_{\alpha \to \infty} H(\alpha) = \log p_i$;
4) $H(1) = H = - \sum_{i=1}^{k} p_i \log p_i$;
5) $\lim_{\alpha \to +\infty} H(\alpha) = \log r$, being r the number of indices j for which p_j has its greatest value
6) $H(\alpha)$ is a convex $\cup$ function.

These properties are schematized in fig. 2.1.

From the properties of $H(\alpha)$ it immediately follows that given any number R, with

$$\log r < R < \log K \tag{2.66}$$

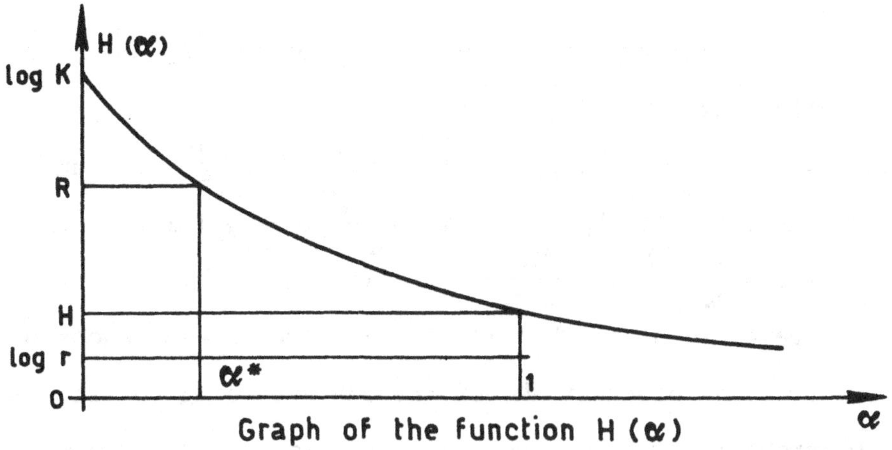

Fig. 2.1

there will exist one and only one number α , say α^* , such that the equation

$$H(\alpha) = R \tag{2.67}$$

is satisfied. Moreover, if

$$H < R < \log K \tag{2.68}$$

then

$$0 < \alpha^* < 1 \tag{2.69}$$

while if

$$\log r < R < H \tag{2.70}$$

then

$$\alpha^* > 1 \tag{2.71}$$

Two additional properties of the $\mathcal{Q}_\alpha$ auxiliary distributions are very important, namely:

1) whenever $p(\underline{u}^{(L)}) \geq p(\underline{v}^{(L)})$, then $q_\alpha(\underline{u}^{(L)}) \geq q_\alpha(\underline{v}^{(L)})$ for any $\alpha>0$;

2) whenever $p(\underline{u}^{(L)}) \geq p(\underline{v}^{(L)})$ then $\frac{p(\underline{u}^{(L)})}{q_\alpha(\underline{u}^{(L)})} > \frac{p(\underline{v}^{(L)})}{q_\alpha(\underline{v}^{(L)})}$ for $0 < \alpha < 1$ while $\frac{p(\underline{u}^{(L)})}{q_\alpha(\underline{u}^{(L)})} < \frac{p(\underline{v}^{(L)})}{q_\alpha(\underline{v}^{(L)})}$ for $\alpha > 1$.

These properties entail that if we order the L-sequences of letters from the alphabet $\mathcal{A}$ of the DMS according to decreasing $\mathcal{P}$-probability, then they are ordered according to decreasing $\mathcal{Q}_\alpha$-probability for every positive α, according to decreasing $\mathcal{P}/\mathcal{Q}_\alpha$ ratio for every α between 0 and 1.

Now we have all the necessary tools for investigating the asymptotic behaviour of the error probability P_e. Assume first that the encoding rate R satisfies eq. (2.68); since $R > H$, we already know that $P_e \downarrow 0$ as $L \to \infty$. Let α^* be the (unique) solution for eqn. (2.67); then α^* lies between zero and one, and for sufficiently small, but otherwise arbitrary, ε the following inequalities hold:

$$H(\alpha^* - \varepsilon) > R > H(\alpha^* + \varepsilon) \tag{2.73}$$

by the decreasing character of the function $H(\alpha)$. Consider the auxiliary distributions $\mathcal{Q}_{\alpha^*-\varepsilon}$ and $\mathcal{Q}_{\alpha^*+\varepsilon}$ defined as in eq (2.63) and let $\mathcal{B}_L^{(R)}$ be the set of the 2^{LR} most $\mathcal{P}$-probable L-length source sequences. In force of property 1) of the auxiliary distribution $\mathcal{B}_L^{(R)}$ is also the set of the 2^{LR} most $\mathcal{Q}_\alpha$-probable sequences.

As a direct consequence of Shannon theorem, inequalities (2.73) imply

$$\mathcal{Q}_{\alpha^*-\varepsilon}(\mathcal{B}_L^{(R)c}) \uparrow 1 \tag{2.74}$$

$$\text{as } L \to \infty$$

$$\mathcal{Q}_{\alpha^*+\varepsilon}(\mathcal{B}_L^{(R)c}) \downarrow 0 \tag{2.75}$$

being $\mathcal{B}_L^{(R)c}$ the complement of $\mathcal{B}_L^{(R)}$.

From (2.74) it follows that for sufficiently large L the set $\mathcal{B}_L^{(R)c}$ satisfies the inequality

$$\mathcal{Q}_{\alpha^*-\varepsilon}(\mathcal{B}_L^{(R)c}) \leqslant 1-\gamma$$

for any fixed γ between zero and one, and therefore

$$\inf_{E^{(L)} \subset \mathcal{A}^L : \mathcal{Q}_{\alpha^*-\varepsilon}(E^{(L)}) \geqslant 1-\gamma} p(E^{(L)}) \leqslant p(\mathcal{B}_L^{(R)c}) \tag{2.76}$$

On the other hand, in force of (2.75), if L is large enough $\mathcal{B}_L^{(R)}$ does not satisfy the inequality

$$\mathcal{Q}_{\alpha^*+\varepsilon}(\mathcal{B}_L^{(R)c}) \geqslant 1-\gamma$$

An application of the Neyman-Pearson lemma with $\mu_2 = \mathcal{P}$, $\mu_1 = \mathcal{Q}_{\alpha^*+\varepsilon}$ and $E_*^{(L)} = \mathcal{B}_L^{(R)c}$ shows that

$$\inf_{E^{(L)} \subset \mathcal{A}^L : \mathcal{Q}_{\alpha^*-\varepsilon}(E^{(L)}) \geqslant 1-\gamma} p(E^{(L)}) \geqslant p(\mathcal{B}_L^{(R)c}) \tag{2.77}$$

Applying theorem 2.3 to the infima appearing in eq.s (11.4) and (11.5) we can deduce

$$(2.78)\qquad \begin{aligned} -I(\mathcal{Q}_{\alpha^*-\varepsilon}\|\mathcal{P}) &\leq \varliminf_{L\to\infty}\frac{1}{L}\log_2 P(\mathcal{B}_L^{(R)}) \leq \\ &\leq \varlimsup_{L\to\infty}\frac{1}{L}\log_2 P(\mathcal{B}_L^{(R)}) \leq -I(\mathcal{Q}_{\alpha^*+\varepsilon}\|\mathcal{P}) \end{aligned}$$

where $P(\mathcal{B}_L^{(R)\,c})$ is actually the probability of incorrect dedoding P_e.

Remark that ε in (2.78) is arbitrarily small and that $I(\mathcal{Q}_\alpha\|\mathcal{P})$ is a continuous function of α ; thus we have proven the following

Theorem 2.8 If the encoding rate R is greater than the entropy H of a DMS operating according to the probability distribution $\mathcal{P} = \{p_1, \ldots, p_2\}$, then the limiting behaviour of the probability of incorrect decoding P_e is as follows:

$$(2.79)\qquad \lim_{L\to\infty}\frac{1}{L}\log_2 P_e = -I(\mathcal{Q}_{\alpha^*}\|\mathcal{P})$$

or also

$$(2.80)\qquad P_e \cong 2^{-LI(\mathcal{Q}_{\alpha^*}\|\mathcal{P})}$$

where $I(\cdot\|\cdot)$ is an I-divergence and $\mathcal{Q}_\alpha$ and α^* are defined in (2.64) and (2.67) respectively.

It is important to observe that if $R < H$, then eq. (2.67) still has a unique solution α^* , but now α^* is greater than 1 , and therefore, in force of property 2 of the auxiliary distribution, ordering the L -sequences according to decreasing $\mathcal{P}$ -probability corresponds to ordering them according to increasing $\mathcal{P}/\mathcal{Q}_{\alpha^*}$ ratio. This entails that in the application of the Neyman-Pearson lemma referred to in eq. (2.77), $\mathcal{B}_L^{(R)c}$ cannot play the role of $E_*^{(L)}$; it is rather $\mathcal{B}_L^{(R)}$ which plays that role. Since in force of eq. (2.73), still valid, we have:

$$\left.\begin{aligned} &\mathcal{Q}_{\alpha^*+\varepsilon}\,(\mathcal{B}_L^{(R)}) \uparrow 1 \\ &\mathcal{Q}_{\alpha^*-\varepsilon}\,(\mathcal{B}_L^{(R)}) \downarrow 0 \end{aligned}\right. \qquad \text{as } L \text{ tends to } \infty$$

we can say that the set $\mathcal{B}_L^{(R)}$ satisfies the inequality $\mathcal{Q}_{\alpha^*+\varepsilon}(\mathcal{B}_L^{(R)}) \geqslant$ $\geqslant 1-\gamma$ for any γ between zero and one and for sufficiently large L , so that

$$\inf_{E^{(L)} \subset \mathcal{A}^L \,:\, \mathcal{Q}_{\alpha^*+\varepsilon} \geqslant 1-\gamma} P(E^{(L)}) \geqslant P(\mathcal{B}_L^{(R)})$$

and on the other side, since the inequality $\mathcal{Q}_{\alpha^*-\varepsilon}\,(\mathcal{B}_L^{(R)}) \geqslant 1-\gamma$ cannot be satisfied for arbitrarily large L , applying the Neyman-Pearson lemma yields:

$$\inf_{E^{(L)} \subset \mathcal{A}^L \,:\, \mathcal{Q}_{\alpha^*-\varepsilon}(\mathcal{B}_L^{(R)}) \geqslant 1-\gamma} P(E^{(L)}) \geqslant P(\mathcal{B}_L^{(R)})$$

Now we remark that $P(\mathcal{B}_L^{(R)}) = 1 - P_e$, and much in the same way as we obtained theorem 2.8 we obtain the following

<u>Theorem 2.9</u> If the encoding rate R is less than the entropy

H of a DMS, then the same notations as in theorem 2.8 the limiting behaviour of the probability of erroneous decoding P_e is as follows:

$$\lim_{L \to \infty} \frac{1}{L} \log_2 (1 - P_e) = - I(\mathcal{Q}_{\alpha^*} \| \mathcal{P})$$

or also

$$P_e \cong 1 - 2^{-LI(\mathcal{Q}_{\alpha^*} \| \mathcal{P})}.$$

Chapter 3

CODING FOR DISCRETE MARKOV SOURCES

3.1. Description of the Markov source.

Consider a finite Markov chain $\mathcal{C}$ having K states $s_1, s_2, \ldots, s_K$ and defined by the initial probability distribution

$$\Pi_0 = \left[p_1 \ldots . p_K \right]^{+)} \tag{3.1}$$

(*) In the sequel Π_0 will often be a degenerate probability distribution, i.e. $p_i = \delta_{ij}$ for some $j (1 \leq i \leq k)$ (Kronecker index).

and by the transition probability matrix

$$\Pi = \begin{bmatrix} p_{11} & p_{12} & \cdots & p_{1k} \\ p_{k1} & p_{k2} & \cdots & p_{kk} \end{bmatrix} . \qquad (3.2)$$

To the chain $\mathcal{C}$ a source $\mathcal{S}$ is associated having an alphabet $\mathcal{A}$ of K letters:

$$\mathcal{A} = \left\{ a_1 , a_2 , \ldots , a_k \right\}$$

and working as follows: when $\mathcal{C}$ goes to state s_i , $\mathcal{S}$ outputs the letter a_i ; the probability of this event depends on the previously emitted letter, say $a_j (1 \leqslant j \leqslant K)$ and coincides with the element p_{ji} of the matrix Π . We can also say that each row of the stochastic matrix Π defines a DMS (Discrete Memoryless Source) $\mathcal{S}_i$ working with the same alphabet $\mathcal{A}$ as $\mathcal{S}$:

$$\mathcal{S}_i = \begin{pmatrix} a_1 & a_2 & \ldots & a_k \\ p_{i1} & p_{i2} & & p_{ik} \end{pmatrix} \qquad (1 \leqslant i \leqslant K). \qquad (3.3)$$

When a letter a_i is output at the k-th step, then $\mathcal{S}_i$ is excited and emits a letter at step $(k + 1)$ according to the finite scheme (3.3); if a_j is emitted by $\mathcal{S}_i$ at step $(k + 1)$, then $\mathcal{S}_j$ is excited and will emit a letter at step $(k + 2)$; and so on.

Consider now a sequence of letters from $\mathcal{S}$ having length n :

$$(3.4) \qquad \underline{u}^{(n)} = (u_0)\, u_1\, u_2 \ldots\, u_n$$

Each u_i belongs to $\mathcal{A}$ and apart from the initial letter u_0, whose value is determined according to Π_0 in (3.1), each of the u_i may be thought of as having been emitted by some DMS, say $\mathcal{S}_i$. We can therefore split $\underline{u}^{(n)}$ into K subsequences $\underline{u}_1$, $\underline{u}_2$, ..., $\underline{u}_k$ as follows:

$$(3.5) \qquad \text{if } u_k = a_i \text{ , then } u_{k+1} \in \underline{u}_i \qquad \begin{pmatrix} 0 \leqslant k \leqslant n-1; \\ i = 1, 2, \ldots, k \end{pmatrix}$$

It is evident that $\underline{u}^{(n)}$ uniquely determines the subsequences $\underline{u}_1$, ..., $\underline{u}_k$; but also, conversely, the $\underline{u}_i$'s together with the initial letter u_0 allow a unique reconstruction of $\underline{u}^{(n)}$.

Adopting this viewpoint in analysing the n-length sequences of $\mathcal{S}$ will enable us to draw several conclusions based upon a kind of independent behaviour of the various DMS's involved. Since the asymptotic behaviour of a DMS is well known, we shall try to make use of the theory of DMS's for investigating Markov sources.

There is no restriction in generality if we assume that

i) the chain $\mathcal{C}$ associated to the source $\mathcal{S}$ is indecomposable; and

ii) there are no periodic states.

Since the chain is finite, assumptions i) and ii) imply ergodicity; therefore one chain has a unique stationary probability distribution, say

$$W = \left[w_1, \ldots , w_k \right] \tag{3.6}$$

and moreover the entropy H of the chain, defined as usual by the limit

$$\lim_{n \to \infty} H(u_n | u_0, u_1, \ldots , u_{n-1}) \tag{3.7}$$

is given by the following expression

$$H = \sum_{1}^{k}{}_i \; w_i \, H_i \tag{3.8}$$

being H_i the entripy of the DMS $\mathcal{S}_i$ i.e.

$$H_i = -\sum_{1}^{k}{}_j \; p_{ij} \; \log p_{ij} \qquad 1 \leqslant i \leqslant K. \tag{3.9}$$

3.2. Typical sequences and well-partioned sequences.

Consider any of the DMS's, $\mathcal{S}_i$ say, associated with $\mathcal{S}$ (cf. 3.3), and consider the (δ_i, n_i)-typical sequences of $\mathcal{S}_i$, i.e. those sequences $\underline{u}_i$ whose probability satisfies

$$\exp_2\left[- n_i(H_i - \delta_i) \right] \geqslant \mathcal{P}_i(\underline{u}_i) \geqslant \exp_2\left[-n_i(H_i + \delta_i) \right] \tag{3.10}$$

where the subscript i in $\mathcal{P}_i$ refers to the i-th row of the matrix Π. The $\mathcal{P}_i$-probability of the set $\mathcal{T}_{(\delta_i, n_i)}$ of the (δ_i, n_i)-typical sequences satisfies in its turn

$$(3.11) \qquad \mathcal{P}_i(\mathcal{T}_{(\delta_i,n_i)}) \geq 1 - \varepsilon_i(\delta_i, n_i)$$

where

$$\lim_{n_i \to \infty} \varepsilon_i(\delta_i, n_i) = 0 \qquad \begin{array}{l} \forall \delta_i > 0 \\ 1 \leq i \leq K. \end{array}$$

The number $M_{(\delta_i, n_i)}$ of typical sequences satisfies:

$$(3.12) \qquad \left[1 - \varepsilon(\delta_i, n_i)\right] 2^{n_i(H_i - \delta_i)} \leq M_{(\delta_i, n_i)} \leq 2^{n_i(H_i + \delta_i)}$$

On the other hand, starting from the entropy H of the given Markov Sources (see (3.8)), we can also define the (δ, n)-typical sequences of $\mathcal{S}$, i.e. those sequences whose probabi lity satisfies:

$$(3.13) \qquad 2^{-n(H-\delta)} \geq \mathcal{P}(\underline{u}) \geq 2^{-n(H+\delta)}$$

being $\mathcal{P}(\underline{u})$ the probability of $\underline{u}$ deduced from matrix Π.

It is well known that the AEP (Asymptotic Equi partition Property) holds also in the Markov case, and this entail that the overall probability of the nontypical sequences goes to zero as $n \to \infty$: if $\mathcal{T}_{(\delta, n)}$ is the typical set, then

$$(3.14) \qquad \mathcal{P}(\mathcal{T}_{(\delta,n)}) \geq 1 - \varepsilon(\delta, n)$$

and

$$\lim_{n \to \infty} \varepsilon(\delta, n) = 0 \qquad \text{for any } \delta > 0 \tag{3.15}$$

Now, if one neglects the initial letter, u_0 of the n -sequence $\underline{u}$ output by $\mathcal{S}$ the $\mathcal{P}$ -probability of $\underline{u}$ is given by

$$\mathcal{P}(\underline{u}) = \mathcal{P}_1(\underline{u}_1), \dots, \mathcal{P}_k(\underline{u}_k) \tag{3.16}$$

where $\underline{u}_1$, ..., $\underline{u}_k$ are the subsequences corresponding to $\underline{u}$.

Of course, neglecting the initial letter u_0 is certainly possible if the initial probability vector is degenerate, which we shall assume to be the case.

Now put $n_i = w_i n$ in (3.10) - (3.12), where w_i is defined in (3.6) Multiplying (3.10) over i from 1 to K by (3.16) we get:

$$2^{-\Sigma_i w_i n \left[H_i - \delta_i\right]} \geq \prod_i \mathcal{P}_i(\underline{u}_i) \geq 2^{-\Sigma_i w_i n \left[H_i + \delta_i\right]} \tag{3.17}$$

or also, by (3.8):

$$2^{-n(H - \Sigma_i w_i \delta_i)} \geq \mathcal{P}(\underline{u}) \geq 2^{-n(H + \Sigma_i w_i \delta_i)}. \tag{3.18}$$

Comparing (3.18) with (3.13) we see that by choosing one (δ_i , n w_i)-typical sequence from each $\mathcal{S}_i$, we can get by suitable combination a (δ , n)-typical sequence of $\mathcal{S}$, where $\delta = \Sigma_i w_i \delta_i$.

The choice $n_i = w_i n$ in (3.10) - (3.12) is some

what arbitrary, but has an important meaning, which we now wish to make clear.

Since the chain is ergodic, the limits

$$\lim_{n \to \infty} p_{ji}^{(n)} = w_i$$

have the following interpretation in terms of the relative frequency of the letters of the Source alphabet $\mathcal{A}$. The rela tive frequency of letter a_i is given by

$$\frac{n_i}{n}, \tag{3.19}$$

being n_i the length of the i-th subsequence $\underline{u}_i$ of $\underline{u}$, as defined above. Then the following theorem is true:

Theorem 3.1 For each letter a_i of $\mathcal{A}$ the relative frequency (3.19) converges in probability to the steady state probability:

$$\lim_{n \to \infty} \text{prob} \frac{n_i}{n} = w_i \qquad (1 \leq i \leq k) \tag{3.20}$$

In Source language, theorem 3.1 above can also be stated as follows: the relative frequency of intervention of the i-th DMS, $\mathcal{S}_i$, in making up an n-length sequence tends in probability to w_i. Of course the relevant probabili ty in (3.20) is the probability deduced from the Π matrix (3.20) of the Markov Source.

After this it is possible to define the (n, ε)-well partioned (WP) sequences for our Source $\mathcal{S}$.

Definition: we say that $\underline{u}^{(n)}$ is (n, ε)-WP if the following inequality holds for every i :

$$\left| \frac{n_i}{n} - w_i \right| < \varepsilon \qquad 1 \leq i \leq k \; , \; \varepsilon > 0 \qquad (3.21)$$

Now Theorem 3.1 and the Definition above entail the following theorem

Theorem 3.2 The overall probability of the (n , ε)-WP sequences tends to 1 as n tends to the infinity for any positive ε .

Now the situation can be described as follows: with probability close to 1 each DMS $\mathcal{S}_i$ emits sequences of length approximately equal to $w_i n$, and at the same time with probability close to 1 each $\mathcal{S}_i$ emits typical sequences. We may therefore conclude that:

with probability close to 1 each DMS $\mathcal{S}_i$ emits typical sequences of length close to $w_i n$.

3.3. The coding problem.

We wish to encode the K^n sequences of length n possibly output by $\mathcal{S}$ by means of a certain number of distinct codewords having all the same length. If we can tolerate a small non-zero probability of erroneous decoding, we can assign codewords to the $\sim 2^{nH}$ typical sequences of length n (each of them being formed by K typical subsequences from the DMS's $\mathcal{S}_i$ of length approximately equal to $w_i n$), while encoding the remaining sequences arbitrarily. Actually the following theorem is true:

Theorem 3.3 If we provide distinct codewords for the 2^{nR} most probable n -length sequences from our Source, then the asymptotic behaviour of the probability of erroneous decoding P_e is as follows:

$$\lim_{n\to\infty} P_e = 0 \qquad \text{if} \quad R > H \tag{3.22}$$

$$\lim_{n\to\infty} P_e = 1 \qquad \text{if} \quad R < H \tag{3.23}$$

being H the entropy of the Source as in (3.8), R is called the "encoding rate".

Theorem 3.3 is a direct consequence of the AEP described by (3.14) and (3.15). Actually let $\mathcal{B}_{n,R}$ be the set of the 2^{nR} most $\mathcal{P}$ -probable (*) n -length sequences; if $R < H$ then the $\sim 2^{nH}$ typical sequences cannot be all contained in $\mathcal{B}_{n,R}$, therefore for sufficiently large n none of them will. On the other hand if $R > H$, then $2^{-nH} > 2^{-nR}$ and therefore the typical sequences are all in $\mathcal{B}_{nR}$ for n large enough. Since $P_e = 1 - \mathcal{P}(\mathcal{B}_{nR})$ theorem 3.3 follows from the AEP.

The above theorem, however, gives no indication about the speed at which P_e goes to zero when $R > H$ or to 1

(*) The somewhat redundant notation $\mathcal{P}$-probable refers to the original matrix Π of the Source; later on other matrices will step in, making this notation useful for avoiding confusion.

when $R > H$. We are therefore in the same situation as for the memoryless case, and we wish to push forward our investigations.

To this end we need some lemmas which are presented in the next section.

3.4. Some auxiliary lemmas.

Consider, along with the stochastic matrix Π in (3.2) another stochastic matrix, say Γ, with elements q_{ij} $(1 \leq i,j \leq k)$, associated to the same alphabet $\mathcal{A}$. Then to any n-sequence $\underline{u}^{(n)}$ two probabilities are associated as follows (as usual we let the initial p.d. be degenerate):

$$\mathcal{P}(\underline{u}) = \mathcal{P}_1(\underline{u}_1) \ldots \mathcal{P}_k(\underline{u}_k) \tag{3.24}$$

$$\mathcal{Q}(\underline{u}) \quad \mathcal{Q}_1(\underline{u}_1) \ldots \mathcal{Q}_k(\underline{u}_k) \tag{3.25}$$

where $\underline{u}_i$ is the subsequence of $\underline{u}$ associated with the DMS $\mathcal{S}_i$ having p.d. equal to the i-th row of Π, $\mathcal{P}_i(\underline{u}_i)$ is the probability of $\underline{u}_i$ according to that p.d. and $\mathcal{Q}_i(\underline{u}_i)$ is the probability of the same subsequence according to the i-th row of matrix Γ. Of course the length n_i of $\underline{u}_i$ tends in $\mathcal{P}$-probability to w_i if Π is the matrix running the Source.

For any set $E \subset \mathcal{A}$ define obviously

(3.26) $$\mathcal{P}(E) = \sum_{\underline{u} \in E} \mathcal{P}(\underline{u}), \quad \mathcal{Q}(E) = \sum_{\underline{u} \in E} \mathcal{Q}(\underline{u}).$$

Lemma 3.1 For any positive δ_i and any index $i (1 \leqslant i \leqslant k)$ define $F_{n w_i}(\delta_i\, w_i)$ as the set made up by those subsequences $\underline{u}_i$ of length $n w_i$ output by the DMS $\mathcal{S}_i$ and satisfying the inequality

(3.27) $$\left| \log \frac{\mathcal{P}_i(\underline{u}_i)}{\mathcal{Q}_i(u_i)} + n w_i M_i \right| < n w_i \delta_i$$

where

(3.28) $$M_i = - \sum_{1}^{k}{}_j\, p_{ij} \log \frac{p_{ij}}{q_{ij}}, \qquad (1 \leqslant i \leqslant k)$$

Then as $n \to \infty$ the $\mathcal{P}$-prob. that $\mathcal{S}_i$ emits a sequence belonging to $F_{n w_i}(\delta_i w_i)$ goes to 1.

Remark that M_i turns out to be just minus an I-divergence

(3.29) $$M_i = - I(\mathcal{P}_i \| \mathcal{Q}_i) \qquad (1 \leqslant i \leqslant k)$$

between the i-th row of Π and the i-th row of Γ. As a consequence $M_i \leqslant 0$.

Proof The $\mathcal{P}$ probability of $\underline{u}^{(n)}$ to be WP tends to one, and by (3.24), the $\mathcal{P}_i$-probability that $\mathcal{S}_i$ emits a sequence $\underline{u}_i$ of length $n w_i$; tends to one. We may therefore restrict our attention to the $(n w_i)$-length sequences from $\mathcal{S}_i$.

Now if we consider all the K^{n_i} sequences $\underline{u}$ of length $n_i = n w_i$ from $\mathcal{A}$ we have

$$\sum_{\underline{u} \in \mathcal{A}^{n_i}} \mathcal{P}(\underline{u}) \log \frac{\mathcal{P}_i(\underline{u})}{\mathcal{Q}_i(\underline{u})} = - n_i M_i \qquad (1 \leqslant i \leqslant k) \quad (3.30)$$

Now Chebichev inequality states that if X is a r.v. then for any positive t

$$\mathcal{P}\left\{ |X| \geqslant t \right\} \leqslant t^{-2} E(X^2)$$

and in particular if $E(X) = \mu$, then

$$P\left\{ |X - \mu| \geqslant t \right\} \leqslant t^{-2} \operatorname{Var}(X). \qquad (3.31)$$

Now let in (3.31) X be $\log \frac{\mathcal{P}_i(\underline{u})}{\mathcal{Q}_i(\underline{u})}$ and t be $n w_i \delta_i$; this yields $\mu = - n_i M_i$ from (3.30). Thus:

$$\mathcal{P}\left\{ \left| \log \frac{\mathcal{P}_i(\underline{u})}{\mathcal{Q}_i(\underline{u})} + n_i M_i \right| \geqslant n w_i \delta_i \right\} \leqslant$$

$$\leqslant \left(\frac{1}{n w_i \delta_i} \right)^2 \sum_{\underline{u} \in \mathcal{A}^{n_i}} \mathcal{P}_i(\underline{u}) \left(\log \frac{\mathcal{P}_i(\underline{u})}{\mathcal{Q}_i(\underline{u})} + n_i M_i \right)^2 = \qquad (3.32)$$

$$= \left(\frac{1}{n w_i \delta_i} \right)^2 n_i \sum_{1}^{k} {}_j \, p_{ij} \left(\log \frac{p_i(\underline{u})}{q_i(\underline{u})} + M_i \right)^2$$

and the last term tends to zero as $n \to \infty$, since $n_i = n w_i$.

Q.d.e.

<u>Remark</u>. By the Markovian dependence between the DMS' $\mathcal{S}_i$, in general $\mathcal{S}_i$ cannot output all the $\mathcal{A}^{n_i}$ sequences

of length n_i : some of them have "operational" probability exactly zero. This is not disturbing since with probability as close to one as we like for n large enough, $\mathcal{S}_i$ will choose a permitted sequence within $F_{nw_i}(\delta_i w_i)$.

Now define $F_n(\delta)$ as the set of the WP sequences $\underline{u}$ of length n from the Markov Source which satisfy the condition

$$\left| \log \frac{\mathcal{P}(\underline{u})}{\mathcal{Q}(\underline{u})} + nM \right| < n\delta \tag{3.33}$$

where $\mathcal{P}(\underline{u})$ and $\mathcal{Q}(\underline{u})$ are defined in (3.24) and (3.25) and M is given by

$$M = \sum_{1}^{k} {}_i \, w_i M_i \tag{3.34}$$

being M defined by (3.28), and δ is any positive numbers.

Then the following lemma is true:

<u>Lemma 3.2</u> The $\mathcal{P}$ -probability that $\mathcal{S}$ emits an n-sequence $\underline{u}$ belonging to $F_n(\delta)$ goes to 1 as $n \to \infty$.

<u>Proof</u> It is clearly sufficient to prove that $F_n(\delta)$ contains a set whose $\mathcal{P}$-probability tends to 1. Such a set is the Cartesian product

$$\Lambda = \prod_{i=1}^{k} F_{nw_i}(w_i \delta_i) \tag{3.35}$$

for suitable values of the δ_i's. Actually by Lemma 3.1 the probability of having a sequence $\underline{u}$ not belonging to Λ is $\mathcal{P}(u) = \prod_{i=1}^{k} \mathcal{P}_i(u_i) \sim 0$ since some of the $\mathcal{P}_i(u_i)$ is arbitrary close to zero. Moreover $F_n(\delta) \supset \Lambda$. Actually since

$$\left| \log \frac{\mathcal{P}(\underline{u})}{\mathcal{Q}(\underline{u})} + nM \right| = \left| \sum_{1}^{k}{}_i \log \frac{\mathcal{P}_i(\underline{u}_i)}{\mathcal{Q}_i(\underline{u}_i)} + n \sum_{1}^{k}{}_i w_i M_i \right| \leq$$

$$\leq \sum_{1}^{k}{}_i \left| \log \frac{\mathcal{P}_i(\underline{u}_i)}{\mathcal{Q}_i(\underline{u}_i)} + n w_i M_i \right| , \tag{3.36}$$

if (3.27) is true for every i , (3.33) is also true for some δ , implying $F_n(\delta) \supset \Lambda$ and the thesis. Q.d.e.

In exactly the same way the following Lemma can be proved where self-explanatory notations have been used:

Lemma 3.2a: The $\mathcal{Q}$-probability that the source corresponding to the stochastic matrix Γ outputs an n-sequence $\underline{u}$ belonging to the set $G_n(\delta)$ of the WP sequences for which

$$\left| \log \frac{\mathcal{Q}(\underline{u})}{\mathcal{P}(\underline{u})} + nM \right| < n\delta$$

where

$$M = \sum_i m_i M_i$$

being $M_i = - I(\mathcal{Q}_i \| \mathcal{P}_i)$ goes to 1 as $n \to \infty$.

Consider now the number

$$B(n, \gamma) = \inf_{E \subset A^n, \mathcal{P}(E^c) < \gamma} \mathcal{Q}(E) \tag{3.37}$$

where γ is any number such that $0<\gamma<1$, E^c is the complementary set of E and $\mathcal{P}(E)$, $\mathcal{Q}(E)$ are defined by (3.24) and (3.25). We are interested in the asymptotic behaviour of $B(n,\gamma)$ as $n \to \infty$, and the following lemma is relevant:

Lemma 3.3 : The asymptotic behaviour of $B(n,\gamma)$ is given by the following limit:

$$\lim_{n\to\infty} \frac{1}{n} \log_2 B(n,\gamma) = M \tag{3.38}$$

being M defined by (3.34) and (3.38)

Proof: By (3.33) if $\underline{u} \in F_n(\delta)$, then

$$\mathcal{Q}(\underline{u})\, 2^{n(-M-\delta)} < \mathcal{P}(\underline{u}) < \mathcal{Q}(\underline{u})\, 2^{-n(-M-\delta)} \tag{3.39}$$

Since by Lemma 3.2 $\mathcal{P}\left(F_n^c(\delta)\right) \to 0$, we have by (3.37) and (3.39)

$$B(n,\gamma) \leqslant \mathcal{Q}\left(F_n(\delta)\right) = \sum_{\underline{u}\in F_n(\delta)} \mathcal{Q}(\underline{u}) \leqslant 2^{n(M+\delta)} \sum_{\underline{u}\in F_n(\delta)} \mathcal{P}(\underline{u}) \tag{3.40}$$

whence

$$B(n,\gamma) \leqslant 2^{n(M+\delta)} \tag{3.41}$$

On the other hand by (3.39) we have also for any $E \subset \mathcal{A}^n$

$$\mathcal{Q}(E) \leqslant \mathcal{Q}\left(E\cap F_n(\delta)\right) \leqslant 2^{n(M-\delta)} \mathcal{P}\left(E\cap F_n(\delta)\right) \tag{3.42}$$

and since $\mathcal{P}(E^c) \geqslant \gamma$ implies $\mathcal{P}\left(E\cap F_n(\delta)\right) \geqslant \frac{1-\gamma}{2}$ for n large enough, from (3.42) we get also

$$B(n,\gamma) \geqslant 2^{n(M-\delta)} \frac{1-\gamma}{2} \tag{3.43}$$

Since in (3.41) and (3.43) δ and γ are arbitrary, these two inequalities yield the thesis. Q.d.e.

If now one defines the number

$$D(n,\gamma) = \min_{E\subset \mathcal{A}^n,\ \mathcal{Q}(E^c)\leq\gamma} \mathcal{P}(E) \tag{3.44}$$

where γ is any number between 0 and 1 , then the following lemma is true:

Lemma 4.3 The asymptotic behaviour of $D(n,\gamma)$ is given by the following limit:

$$\lim_{n\to\infty} \frac{1}{n} \log D(n,\gamma) = N \tag{3.45}$$

where N is defined by

$$N = \sum_i \mu_i N_i \tag{3.46}$$

being now $\{\mu_i\}$ the stationary distribution (*) of matrix Γ and N_i is given by

$$N_i = -\sum_{1}^{k}{}_j\, q_{ij} \log \frac{q_{ij}}{p_{ij}} = -I(\mathcal{Q}_i\|\mathcal{P}_i) \tag{3.47}$$

$$(1 \leq i \leq k)$$

(*) We assume of course that Γ is an irriducible ergodic stochastic matrix.

3.5. Application to the number of distinct codewords.

As a first application of the foregoing to the coding problems, consider the following question: assume a given level for the probability of erroneous decoding, $\bar{P}_e$ say, should not be overcome; what is then the minimal number of distinct codewords that should be provided?

Take as an auxiliary matrix the following one

$$\Gamma = \left\| \begin{array}{ccc} \frac{1}{k} & \cdots & \frac{1}{k} \\ \hline \frac{1}{k} & \cdots & \frac{1}{k} \end{array} \right\| \tag{3.48}$$

Consequently for any n-length sequence $\underline{u}$ the corresponding $\mathcal{Q}$-probability is:

$$\mathcal{Q}(\underline{u}) = \frac{1}{k^n} \tag{3.49}$$

and for any $E \subset \mathcal{A}$ having $|E|$ elements

$$\mathcal{Q}(E) = \frac{|E|}{k^n} \tag{3.50}$$

Consequently for this particular matrix Γ the quantity $B(n,\gamma)$ in (3.37) gives us a quantity proportional to the smallest number of elements contained in a set $E \subset \mathcal{A}^n$ whose complementary E^c satisfies the limitation $\mathcal{P}(E^c) < \gamma$.

As a direct consequence of Lemma 3 above we have the following

Theorem 3.4 To achieve an arbitrarily small probability of erroneous decoding in a fixed-length encoding scheme, one cannot use less than

$$\mathcal{N} = 2^{nH}$$

distinct codewords, where H is the source entropy as defined by (3.8).

Proof: For this particular choice of Γ, eq. (3.38) specializes as follows:

$$\lim_{n \to \infty} \frac{1}{n} \log B(n, \gamma) = \Sigma_i w_i \left| - \Sigma_j p_{ij} \log p_{ij} k \right| \quad (3.51)$$

whence for large n

$$B(n, \gamma) \cong \frac{2^{n \Sigma_i w_i H_i}}{K^n} = \frac{2^{nH}}{K^n} . \quad (3.52)$$

The thesis now follows from (3.48) multiplying both sides by K^n and taking into account (3.46).

This result can also be stated as follows:

Theorem 3.5 If we encode the source sequences of length n using distinct codewords for the $\sim 2^{nH}$ typical sequences, then we can keep the probability of erroneous decoding under any specified level, provided n is large enough. On the other hand if less than $\sim 2^{nH}$ distinct codewords are provided, this is not possible, rather the error probability goes to 1 as $n \to \infty$.

This is once more Shannon's theorem.

Of course one is reasonably led to assign the $2^{nR(*)}$ distinct codewords at hand to the 2^{nR} most $\mathcal{P}$-prob able sequences rather than to 2^{nR} sequences having probability $\sim 2^{-nH}$. But actually there is no difference between the two encoding schemes, since the non typical sequences more probable than $\sim 2^{-nH}$ are in a negligibly small number if compared with 2^{nH} and a fortiori with $2^{n \log K}$

Chapter 4

THE ERROR EXPONENT

4.1. The auxiliary distribution.

Now we shall apply to the case of the MS a method used by Csiszár and Longo in the case of a DMS. We shall prove the exponential behaviour of $P_e^{(n)}$, without being able, however, to find the expression for the exponent. Further investigation on this will be carried out in the sequel.

Consider any fixed n and let us introduce in the set of the K^n n-sequences an auxiliary p.d. $\mathcal{Q}_\alpha$, defined as follows:

$$\mathcal{Q}_\alpha(\underline{u}^{(n)}) = \mathcal{P}^\alpha(\underline{u})/A_n(\alpha) \tag{4.1}$$

where α is a positive parameter to be specified later and $A_n(\alpha)$ is a normalizing factor:

$$A_n(\alpha) = \sum_{\underline{u}^{(n)}} \mathcal{P}^\alpha(\underline{u}^{(n)}) \tag{4.2}$$

It is to be remarked that if α is not equal to 1 or to 0 the auxiliary distribution does not define a process, since if we sum the $\mathcal{Q}_\alpha(\underline{u}^{(n+1)})$-probability of the K $(n+1)$-sequences obtained from a fixed n-sequence $\underline{u}^{(n)}$ by adding one more letter, we do not obtain $\mathcal{Q}_\alpha(\underline{u}^{(n)})$:

$$\sum \mathcal{Q}_\alpha(\underline{u}^{(n+1)}) \neq \mathcal{Q}_\alpha(\underline{u}^{(n)}) \tag{4.3}$$

In spite of this, however, many interesting conclusions can be drawn. First of all a kind of law of large numbers holds, and to arrive at it we shall use Cebicev's inequality in the form

$$\text{(4.4)} \qquad \text{Prob}\left\{|x - \bar{x}| > \varepsilon\right\} < \frac{\sigma^2}{\varepsilon^2}$$

where $\bar{x}$ and σ^2 are the mean value and the variance of the r.v. x respectively, and ε is a positive constant. Take now $\frac{1}{n}\log \mathcal{P}(\underline{u}^{(n)})$ instead of x and take as probability distribution the auxiliary p.d. $\mathcal{Q}_\alpha$; then (4.4) yields

$$\mathcal{Q}_\alpha\left\{\left|\frac{1}{n}\log\mathcal{P}(\underline{u}^{(n)}) - \frac{1}{n}E_{\mathcal{Q}_\alpha}\left(\log\mathcal{P}(\underline{u}^{(n)})\right)\right| \geq \varepsilon\right\} =$$

$$\text{(4.5)} \qquad = \mathcal{Q}_\alpha\left\{\left|\log\mathcal{P}(\underline{u}^{(n)}) - E_{\mathcal{Q}_\alpha}\left(\log\mathcal{P}(\underline{u}^{(n)})\right)\right| \geq n\varepsilon\right\} < \frac{1}{\varepsilon^2 n^2}\text{Var}\left(\log\mathcal{P}(\underline{u}^{(n)})\right)$$

We can therefore conclude, passing to the limit as $n \to \infty$, that if the limit

$$\text{(4.6)} \qquad \lim_{n\to\infty}\frac{1}{n}E_{\mathcal{Q}_\alpha}\left(\log\mathcal{P}(\underline{u}^{n})\right)$$

exists and if

$$\text{(4.7)} \qquad \lim_{n\to\infty}\frac{1}{n^2}\text{Var}_{\mathcal{Q}_\alpha}\left(\log\mathcal{P}(\underline{u}^{(n)})\right) = 0$$

then a sort of "asymptotic equipartition property" (AEP) holds, i.e. with "great" $\mathcal{Q}_\alpha$ -probability an n-sequence satisfies

$$\frac{1}{n}\log\mathcal{P}(\underline{u}^{(n)}) \simeq \frac{1}{n}E_{\mathcal{Q}_\alpha}\left(\log\mathcal{P}(\underline{u}^{(n)})\right)$$

The proof of the AEP is essentially based on the following inequalities, which are very easily checked:

$$\frac{d}{d\alpha} \log A_n(\alpha) = E_{\mathcal{Q}_\alpha}\left(\log \mathcal{P}(\underline{u}^{(n)})\right) \tag{4.9}$$

$$\frac{d^2}{d\alpha^2} \log A_n(\alpha) = \mathrm{Var}_{\mathcal{Q}_\alpha}\left(\log \mathcal{P}(\underline{u}^{(n)})\right) \tag{4.10}$$

and on an argument due to Koopmans, who has shown that the limits

$$\lim_{n\to\infty} \frac{1}{n} \log A_n(\alpha) \tag{4.11}$$

$$\lim_{n\to\infty} \frac{1}{n} \frac{d}{d\alpha} \log A_n(\alpha) \tag{4.11'}$$

$$\lim_{n\to\infty} \frac{1}{n} \frac{d^2}{d\alpha^2} \log A_n(\alpha) \tag{4.11''}$$

all exist, implying the AEP by (4.9), (4.6), (4.10) and (4.7).

Let us consider next the entropy $H_n(\alpha)$ of the auxiliary distribution $\mathcal{Q}_\alpha$ on the set of the n-sequences:

$$H_n(\alpha) = -\sum_{\underline{u}^{(n)}} \mathcal{Q}_\alpha(\underline{u}^{(n)}) \log \mathcal{Q}_\alpha(\underline{u}^{(n)}) \tag{4.12}$$

On account of (3.1) $H_n(\alpha)$ has the following expression:

$$H_n(\alpha) = \log A_n(\alpha) - \alpha E_{\mathcal{Q}_\alpha}\left(\log \mathcal{P}(\underline{u}^{(n)})\right) \tag{4.13}$$

now, dividing both sides by n and taking into account (4.9), one gets the following form for the entropy per letter for the n -sequences:

$$\frac{1}{n} H_n(\alpha) = \frac{1}{n} \log A_n(\alpha) - \alpha \frac{1}{n} \frac{d}{d\alpha} \log A_n(\alpha) \tag{4.14}$$

By (4.11)'s the limit

$$\lim_{n\to\infty} \frac{1}{n} H_n(\alpha) = H(\alpha) \tag{4.15}$$

exists and can be considered as the limiting entropy per letter. It is to be observed that for each value of n the entropy per letter $\frac{1}{n} H_n(\alpha)$ is a strictly decreasing function of α and therefore also its limit $H(\alpha)$ is such a function.

Therefore the arguments available in the memoryless case can be used also in the Markov case, the only difference being that in the memoryless case the I -divergence between two p.d.s μ_1 and μ_2 exhibits the following property:

$$I(\mu_1 \| \mu_2 ; n) = n\, I(\mu_1 \| \mu_2 ; 1) \tag{4.16}$$

where $I(\mu_1 \| \mu_2 ; 1)$ is the usual I -divergence, i.e. under one sample of observation and $I(\mu_1 \| \mu_2 ; n)$ is the I -divergence between μ_1 and μ_2 under n (independent) samples. In the Markovian case property (4.16) is no longer true, since the n successive samples are not independent, and consequently it is not possible to compute the limit

$$\lim_{n\to\infty} \frac{1}{n} I(\mu_1 \| \mu_2 ; n) \tag{4.17}$$

in a straightforward way.

The result, however, is expressed by the following

Theorem 4.1 If the encoding rate R is greater than the entropy H of a finite ergodic MS, then the limiting behaviour of the error probability $P_e^{(n)}$ is given by

$$-\lim_{n\to\infty}\frac{1}{n}I(\mathcal{Q}_{\alpha'+\varepsilon}\|\mathcal{P};n)\leq\lim_{n\to\infty}\frac{1}{n}\log P_e^{(n)}\leq-\lim_{n\to\infty}\frac{1}{n}I(\mathcal{Q}_{\alpha'-\varepsilon}\|\mathcal{P};n) \tag{4.18}$$

where α' is the unique solution of the equation in α

$$H_n(\alpha) = R$$

and depends clearly on n, and ε is a sufficiently small but otherwise arbitrary positive number; $I(\cdot\|\cdot;n)$ means that the I -divergence is computed between two p.d.s on the set of all the K^n -sequences.

Theorem 4.1 shows an exponential behaviour of $P_e^{(n)}$ but on the other hand gives us no explicit expression for the exponent.

Using once more the same techniques as in the memoryless case, also the following theorem can be proven:

Theorem 4.2 If the encoding rate R is smaller than the entropy H of the MS, then the limiting behaviour of $P_e^{(n)}$ is

$$-\lim_{n\to\infty}\frac{1}{n}I(\mathcal{Q}_{\alpha'+\varepsilon}\|\mathcal{P};n)\leq\lim_{n\to\infty}\frac{1}{n}\log\left[1-P_e^{(n)}\right]\leq-\lim_{n\to\infty}\frac{1}{n}I(\mathcal{Q}_{\alpha'-\varepsilon}\|\mathcal{P};n). \tag{4.19}$$

We do not intend to give the proof of theorems 4.1 and 4.2, which can be derived from the analogous proof for the memoryless case. We only mention that the proof strongly relies on the techniques used for testing statistical hypotheses, and especially on the Neyman-Pearson lemma. We point out that this approach is essentially easier than Koopman's, although much less general.

4.2. The auxiliary stochastic matrix.

There is an alternative possibility for studying the asymptotic behaviour of the error probability for a Markov Source, based on the introduction of an auxiliary stochastic matrix. Of course the auxiliary matrix induces a p.d. on the n - tuples, and this p.d. induces a process, contrary to the p.d. introduced in 4.1.

It is readily seen that the only possible form for the auxiliary matrix is the following

$$\Gamma(\alpha_1, \dots, \alpha_k) = \Gamma(\bar{\alpha}) = \begin{bmatrix} \frac{p_{11}^{\alpha_1}}{A_1} & \frac{p_{12}^{\alpha_1}}{A_1} & \cdots & \frac{p_{1k}^{\alpha_1}}{A_1} \\ \frac{p_{21}^{\alpha_2}}{A_2} & \frac{p_{22}^{\alpha_2}}{A_2} & \cdots & \frac{p_{2k}^{\alpha_2}}{A_2} \\ \dots & \dots & \dots & \dots \\ \frac{p_{k1}^{\alpha_k}}{A_k} & \frac{p_{k2}^{\alpha_k}}{A_k} & \cdots & \frac{p_{kk}^{\alpha_k}}{A_k} \end{bmatrix} \tag{4.20}$$

where the p_{ij}'s are the elements of Π and the A_i's are normalizing factors:

$$A_i = \Sigma_j \, p_{ij}^{\alpha_i} \qquad (1 \leq i \leq k) \qquad (4.21)$$

and $\bar{\alpha} = (\alpha_1, \alpha_2, \ldots, \alpha_k)$ is a nonnegative vector (i.e. its components are all nonnegative).

Let $\mathcal{Q}_{\bar{\alpha}}(\underline{u}^{(n)})$ be the probability of the sequence $\underline{u}^{(n)}$ induced by $\Gamma(\bar{\alpha})$. With self-evident notation, according to the splitting of $\underline{u}^{(n)}$ into subsequences as shown in (2.4), we shall write

$$\mathcal{P}(\underline{u}^{(n)}) = \prod_{i=1}^{k} \mathcal{P}_i(\underline{u}_i^{(n_i)}) \qquad (\Sigma_i \, n_i = n) \qquad (4.22)$$

$$\mathcal{Q}_{\bar{\alpha}}(\underline{u}^{(n)}) = \prod_{i=1}^{k} \mathcal{Q}_i(\underline{u}_i^{(n_i)}) \qquad (\Sigma_i \, n_i = n) \qquad (4.23)$$

being $\mathcal{P}_i(.)$ and $\mathcal{Q}_i(.)$ the probabilities of the subsequences $\underline{u}^{(n_i)}$ as given by the i-th row of Π and $\Gamma(\bar{\alpha})$ respectively.

The K-dimensional vectors $\bar{\alpha}$ can be partially ordered in an obvious way: $\bar{\alpha}_1$ is "greater" than $\bar{\alpha}_2$ if no component of $\bar{\alpha}_1$ is smaller than the corresponding component of $\bar{\alpha}_2$.

Remark that $\Gamma(\bar{\alpha})$ coincides with Π if the K components of $\bar{\alpha}$ are 1. Moreover $\Gamma(\bar{\alpha})$ is an ergodic stochastic matrix if Π is, for each choice of nonnegative components $\alpha_i \, (1 \leq i \leq k)$ of $\bar{\alpha}$, and consequently $\Gamma(\bar{\alpha})$ possesses a unique stationary and invariant p.d. which obviously depends on $\bar{\alpha}$, say

$$(4.24) \qquad M(\bar{\alpha}) = \left\{ m_1(\bar{\alpha}),\ m_2(\bar{\alpha}), \ldots, m_k(\bar{\alpha}) \right\}$$

As a consequence the entropy $H(\bar{\alpha})$ of the MS corresponding to $\Gamma(\bar{\alpha})$ has the following expression:

$$(4.25) \qquad H(\bar{\alpha}) = \sum_{1}^{k}{}_i \ m_i(\bar{\alpha}) \ H_i(\alpha_i)$$

where $H_i(\alpha_i)$ is the entropy of the p.d. $\mathcal{Q}_{\alpha_i}$ corresponding to the i-th row of $\Gamma(\bar{\alpha})$

We shall be interested in the behaviour of $H(\bar{\alpha})$ as a function of $\bar{\alpha}$. As a first remark in this direction, we note than the components of $M(\bar{\alpha})$ are rational functions of each component of $\bar{\alpha}$: this follows immediately from the invariant character of $M(\bar{\alpha})$:

$$(4.26) \qquad M(\bar{\alpha}) = M(\bar{\alpha}) \cdot \Gamma(\bar{\alpha})$$

(consider the components $m_i(\bar{\alpha})$ as unknowns in the system of linear equations (4.26)). Next we prove the following

<u>Lemma 4.1</u> The entropy $H(\bar{\alpha})$ defined by (4.25) is a strictly decreasing function in the partially ordered set of the vectors $\bar{\alpha}$.

<u>Proof</u>. Each function $H_i(\alpha_i)$ is a strictly decreasing function of α_i taking the value $\log K$ for $\alpha_i=0$ and the value H_i (entropy of $\mathcal{P}_i$) for $\alpha_i = 1$. On the other hand it is not possible to describe in simple terms the variation of $m_i(\bar{\alpha})$ when $\bar{\alpha}$ varies, since the condition

$$\Sigma_i \, m_i(\bar{\alpha}) = 1 \tag{4.27}$$

must be satisfied for each $\bar{\alpha}$. Consequently $H(\bar{\alpha})$ is a weighted mean of decreasing functions, where the weights however change in an unpredictable way. Let $\bar{\alpha}^*$ be any point having positive components (if $\bar{\alpha}^*$ is the null K -tuple the Lemma is trivially true) and let $\bar{\alpha}_j^*$ be a point obtained form $\bar{\alpha}^*$ by increasing its j -th component by a positive quantity ε_j :

$$\bar{\alpha}^* = (\bar{\alpha}_1^*, \bar{\alpha}_2^*, \ldots, \bar{\alpha}_j^*, \ldots, \bar{\alpha}_k^*), \quad \bar{\alpha}_j^* = (\bar{\alpha}_1^*, \bar{\alpha}_2^*, \ldots, \bar{\alpha}_j^* + \varepsilon_j, \ldots, \bar{\alpha}_k^*) \tag{4.28}$$

We wish to prove that if ε_j is sufficiently small, then $H(\bar{\alpha}_j^*) < H(\bar{\alpha}^*)$ $(1 \leqslant j \leqslant k)$.

Actually consider the difference $H(\bar{\alpha}_j^*) - H(\bar{\alpha}^*)$:

$$H(\bar{\alpha}_j^*) - H(\bar{\alpha}^*) = \sum_{i \neq j} m_i(\bar{\alpha}_j^*) H_i(\bar{\alpha}_i^*) + m_j(\bar{\alpha}_j^*) H_j(\bar{\alpha}_j^* + \varepsilon_j) -$$

$$- \sum_{i \neq j} m_i(\bar{\alpha}^*) H_i(\bar{\alpha}_i^*) - m_j(\bar{\alpha}^*) H_j(\bar{\alpha}_j^*) = \sum_{i \neq j} \Big[m_i(\bar{\alpha}_j^*) -$$

$$- m_i(\bar{\alpha}^*) \Big] H_i(\bar{\alpha}_i^*) + m_j(\bar{\alpha}_j^*) \Big[H_j(\bar{\alpha}_j^*) - h_j \Big] - m_j(\bar{\alpha}^*) H_j(\bar{\alpha}_j^*)$$

since $H_j(\alpha_j)$ is decreasing in α_j^* and therefore $H(\alpha_j^*) = H_j(\alpha_j^* + \varepsilon_j) + h_j$ with $h_j > 0$. Moreover for each index i :

$$m_i(\bar{\alpha}_j^*) \cong m_i(\bar{\alpha}^*) + \frac{\partial m_i(\bar{\alpha}^*)}{\partial \alpha_j} \varepsilon_j$$

and therefore for sufficiently small ε_j:

$$H(\bar{\alpha}_j^*) - H(\bar{\alpha}^*) = \varepsilon_j \sum_{i \neq j} H_i(\bar{\alpha}_i^*) \frac{\partial m_i(\bar{\alpha}^*)}{\partial \alpha_i} + \varepsilon_j H_j(\bar{\alpha}_j^*) \frac{\partial m_j(\bar{\alpha}^*)}{\partial \alpha_j} -$$

$$- h_j m_j(\bar{\alpha}_j^*) = \varepsilon_j \sum_i \frac{\partial m_i(\bar{\alpha}^*)}{\partial \alpha_j} H_i(\bar{\alpha}_i^*) - h_j m_j(\bar{\alpha}_j^*)$$

On the other hand by (4.27) in each point $\bar{\alpha}$:

$$\sum_i \frac{\partial m_i(\bar{\alpha})}{\partial \alpha_j} = 0 \qquad (1 < j < k)$$

and therefore

$$\sum_i \frac{\partial m_i(\bar{\alpha}^*)}{\partial \alpha_j} H_i(\alpha_i^*) \leqslant \max_i H_i(\alpha_i^*) \sum_i \frac{\partial m_i(\bar{\alpha}^*)}{\partial \alpha_j} = 0$$

which proves the Lemma, since ε_j is positive and $m_j(\bar{\alpha}_j^*)$ is positive too. Q.d.e.

The following picture illustrates the behaviour of the $H_i(\alpha_i)$ functions if we assume $H_1 > H_2 > \ldots > H_k$.

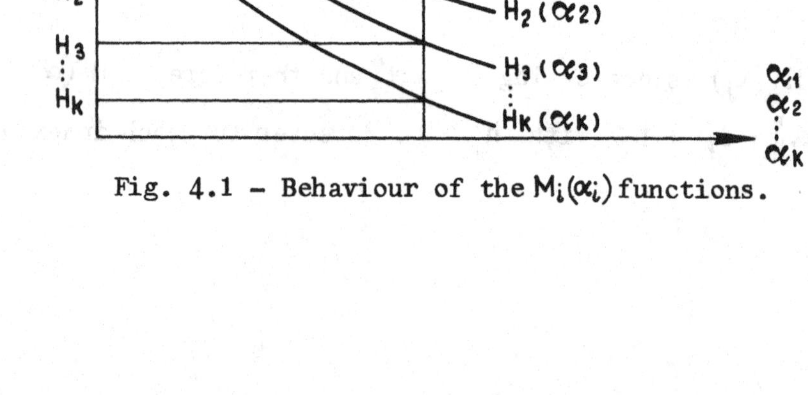

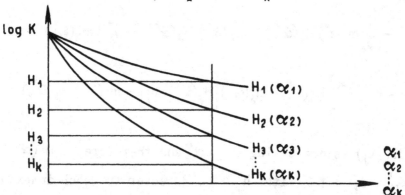

Fig. 4.1 – Behaviour of the $M_i(\alpha_i)$ functions.

4.3. A lower bound on the error probability.

Our problem is to estimate the exponent of $P_e^{(n)}$ which is the probability of error relative to encoding the n - length sequences output by the MS.

Now reconsider the function $H(\bar{\alpha})$ defined by (4.25). In addition to the decreasing character shown by Lemma 4.1 $H(\bar{\alpha})$ has the following properties: it is continuous relative to each of its arguments: it takes on the value $\log K$ when $\bar{\alpha} = (0,0,\dots,0)$ and the value H defined in (3.8) when $\bar{\alpha} = (1, 1,\dots, 1)$. As a consequence, given an encoding rate R such that

$$\log K > R > H \tag{4.29}$$

the equation in the unknown vector $\bar{\alpha}$

$$H(\bar{\alpha}) \tag{4.30}$$

will have solutions $\bar{\alpha}$ satisfying

$$(0,0,\dots,0) < \bar{\alpha} < (1,1,\dots,1) \tag{4.31}$$

where the double vector inequality in (4.31) is to be understood on every component of $\bar{\alpha}$. Each of the solutions $\bar{\alpha}$ of eq. (4.30) defines a stochastic matrix $\Gamma(\bar{\alpha})$, whose entropy is exactly R. Moreover, by the inequality on the right in eq. (4.31), the entropy $H_i(\alpha_i)$ of the i-th row of such a $\Gamma(\bar{\alpha})$ is greater than the entropy H_i of the corresponding row of Π (cfr. Figure 4.1):

(4.32) $$H_i(\alpha_i) > H_i \qquad (1 \leq i \leq k)$$

Let $\mathcal{E}_R$ be the set of vectors $\bar{\alpha}$ satisfying both (4.31) and (4.32) for a fixed value of R satisfying (4.29). We remark that conditions (4.32) seem to be necessary for $P_e^{(n)}$ to vanish as $n \to \infty$; actually this approach roughly corresponds to a splitting of R into K "partial rates" $R_1, R_2, \ldots, R_k$ with

(4.33) $$R_i = H_i(\alpha_i) \qquad (1 \leq i \leq k)$$

being α_i the i-th component of any solution of (4.30) satisfying (4.32). In other words, each DMS making up the DMS Π is given an encoding rate R_i, which should be greater than the corresponding entropy H_i.

Let now $\bar{\alpha}$ be any vector in $\mathcal{E}_R$ and $\bar{\varepsilon}$ a nonnegative vector having at least one positive component: since $H(\bar{\alpha}) = R$ and $H(\bar{\alpha})$ is decreasing, we have

(4.34) $$H(\bar{\alpha} - \bar{\varepsilon}) > R$$

and therefore for every n

(4.35) $$2^{nH(\bar{\alpha} - \bar{\varepsilon})} > 2^{nR}$$

Now 2^{nR} is just the number of n-sequences contained in the set $\mathcal{B}_{n,R}$ defined just after Theorem 3.3, while $2^{nH(\bar{\alpha} - \bar{\varepsilon})}$ is approximately the number of "typical sequences" corresponding to the matrix $\Gamma(\bar{\alpha}-\bar{\varepsilon})$ (the typical sequences have a probability $\sim 2^{-nH(\bar{\alpha}-\bar{\varepsilon})}$) and their overall probability is ~ 1). This implies that the $\mathcal{Q}_{\bar{\alpha}-\bar{\varepsilon}}$ -probability of the sets $\mathcal{B}_{n,R}$ tends to zero, or equivalently

$$\lim_{n\to\infty} \mathcal{Q}_{\bar{\alpha}-\bar{\varepsilon}}(\mathcal{B}^c_{n,R}) = 1 \tag{4.36}$$

and therefore for any fixed $\beta(0<\beta<1)$ the inequality

$$\mathcal{Q}_{\bar{\alpha}-\bar{\varepsilon}}(\mathcal{B}^c_{n,R}) \geqslant \beta \tag{4.37}$$

will be satisfied for n large enough: as a consequence

$$P_e^{(n)} = \mathcal{P}(\mathcal{B}^c_{n,R}) \leqslant \min_{E^{(n)}\subset \mathcal{A}^n,\ \mathcal{Q}_{\bar{\alpha}-\bar{\varepsilon}}(E^{(n)c})<\beta} \mathcal{P}(E^{(n)}) \tag{4.38}$$

By Lemma 4.3 applied when $\mathcal{Q}$ is replaced by $\mathcal{Q}_{\bar{\alpha}-\bar{\varepsilon}}$ we conclude that

$$\lim_{n\to\infty} \frac{1}{n} \log P_e^{(n)} \leqslant M \tag{4.39}$$

where now M is given by

$$M = -\sum_1^k{}_i\ m_i(\bar{\alpha}-\bar{\varepsilon})\ I(\mathcal{Q}_{\bar{\alpha}-\bar{\varepsilon}}\|\mathcal{P}_i) \tag{4.40}$$

In (4.40) obviously $m_i(\bar{\alpha}-\bar{\varepsilon})$ is the i -th element of the invariant p.d. of $\Gamma(\bar{\alpha}-\bar{\varepsilon})$ and $I(\mathcal{Q}_{\bar{\alpha}-\bar{\varepsilon},i}\|\mathcal{P}_i)$ is the I -divergence between the i -th row of $\Gamma(\bar{\alpha}-\bar{\varepsilon})$ and the i -th row of Π . Letting I_i indicate this I -divergence, since $\bar{\varepsilon}$ has components arbitrarily close to zero, from (4.39) we get:

$$(2.41)\quad P_e^{(n)} > 2^{-n\sum_1^k m_i(\bar{\alpha}) I_i} \qquad (\bar{\alpha} \in \mathcal{C}_R)$$

whence, letting $\bar{\alpha}$ vary in $\mathcal{C}_R$, also

$$(2.42)\quad P_e^{(n)} > \sup_{\bar{\alpha} \in \mathcal{C}_R} 2^{-n\sum_1^k m_i(\bar{\alpha}) I_i}$$

which is the desired form of the lower bound.

4.4. Considerations on the upper bound. A conjecture.

Consider again the vectors $\bar{\alpha}$ (belonging to $\mathcal{C}_R$) and $\bar{\varepsilon}$ appearing in inequality (4.34), and let now $\Gamma(\bar{\alpha} + \bar{\varepsilon})$ be the auxiliary matrix: of course

$$(2.43)\quad H(\bar{\alpha} + \bar{\varepsilon}) < R$$

Fix any real number β between zero and one, and order the n - sequences according to decreasing ratio $\mathcal{P}(\underline{u})/\mathcal{Q}'(\underline{u})$ where $\mathcal{Q}'(.)$ stands now for the probability induced by $\Gamma(\bar{\alpha} + \bar{\varepsilon})$. Let $\mathcal{F}_n$ be the set formed by as many sequences -taken in that order- as are necessary for having

$$(2.44)\quad \mathcal{Q}'(\mathcal{F}_n) = \beta$$

Now Theorem 2.5 or Theorem 2.6 can be stated in the following way:

If $E_*^{(n)} \subset \mathcal{A}$ is a set such that $\mathcal{P}(E_*^{(n)}) = 1 - \gamma$

$(0 < \gamma < 1)$ and if $\underline{v}^{(n)} \notin E_*^{(n)}$ implies

$$\frac{\mathcal{P}(\underline{v}^{(n)})}{\mathcal{Q}'(\underline{v}^{(n)})} > \sup_{\underline{u} \in E_*^{(n)}} \frac{\mathcal{P}(\underline{u})}{\mathcal{Q}'(\underline{u})}$$

then

$$\mathcal{P}(E_*^{(n)}) = D(n,\gamma)$$

where $D(n,\gamma)$ is defined by eq. (3.44). As a direct consequence of this form of the Neyman-Pearson Lemma we have the following

Proposition 4.1 The $\mathcal{P}$ -probability (induced by Π) of the set $\mathcal{F}_n^c$ achieves the minimum $D(n,\beta)$, and consequently by Lemma 4.3 for n large enough:

$$\mathcal{P}(\mathcal{F}_n^c) \cong 2^{nM} \tag{4.45}$$

where

$$M = -\sum_1^k{}_i\, m_i I_i \tag{4.46}$$

being $\{m_i\}$ the stationary p.d. for $\Gamma(\bar{\alpha} + \bar{\varepsilon})$ and I_i the I -divergence between the i -th row of $\Gamma(\bar{\alpha} + \bar{\varepsilon})$ and the i -th row of Π .

We remark explicitly that $\mathcal{F}_n^c$ does not coincide with the complementary $\mathcal{B}_{n,R}^c$ of the set $\mathcal{B}_{n,R}^c$ formed by the 2^{nR} most $\mathcal{P}$ -probable sequences, and therefore Proposition 4.1 does not permit to draw any conclusion on $\mathcal{P}_e^{(n)}$; it permits however to draw several conclusions on $\mathcal{F}_n$.

Corollary 4.1 The number $|\mathfrak{F}_n|$ of elements contained in $\mathfrak{F}_n$ increases exponentially with an exponent S which satisfies

(4.47) $$|\mathfrak{F}_n| \cong 2^{nS} > 2^{nH}$$

Proof Since $\mathcal{P}(\mathfrak{F}_n)\uparrow 1$ by Proposition 4.1, the $\sim 2^{nH}$ $\mathcal{P}$-typical sequences should be contained in $\mathfrak{F}_n$ asymptotically. On the other hand the $\mathcal{P}$ -probability of a set ($\mathfrak{F}_n$ in this case) can be arbitrarily small iff the complementary set ($\mathfrak{F}_n$) contains at least 2^{nH} sequences. Q.d.e.

Corollary 4.2 The smallest $\mathcal{P}/\mathcal{Q}$ ratio for a sequence belonging to $\mathfrak{F}_n$ is approximately 2^{nM} .

Proof By Lemma 3.2a the $\mathcal{Q}'$ probability of the sequences for which $\mathcal{P}/\mathcal{Q}' \cong 2^{nH}$ tends to 1 when $n \to \infty$. On the other hand also the set of the $\mathcal{Q}'$ -typical sequences for which $\mathcal{Q}' \cong 2^{-nH(\bar{\alpha}+\bar{\varepsilon})}$ has a $\mathcal{Q}'$ -probability going to 1 . Therefore the intersection of these two sets has the same property: but the intersection must be contained partly in $\mathfrak{F}_n$ and partly in $\mathfrak{F}_n^c$, since $\mathcal{Q}'(\mathfrak{F}_n) = \beta < 1$ for every n . Since the sequences in $\mathfrak{F}_n$ are arranged according to decreasing $\mathcal{P}/\mathcal{Q}'$ ratio, the thesis follows.

Q.d.e.

Now remark that the rate S appearing in inequality (4.47) actually depends on $\bar{\alpha}$, because the set $\mathfrak{F}_n$ itself does: $\mathfrak{F}_n = \mathfrak{F}_n(\bar{\alpha})$. Moreover, the relevant comparison is between the rate $S(\bar{\alpha})$ and the encoding rate R . It may happen that for some of the vectors $\bar{\alpha}$ belonging to $\mathfrak{C}_R$, $S(\bar{\alpha})$ is not greater than R . Let $\mathcal{E}_R^* \subset \mathcal{E}_R$ be such a set. Then we can state and prove the following

<u>Theorem 4.1</u> If there exists a nonempty set $\mathcal{E}_R^* \subset \mathcal{E}_R$ such that

$$S(\bar{\alpha}) < R \tag{4.48}$$

whenever $\bar{\alpha} \in \mathcal{E}_R^*$, then the following upperbound on $P_e^{(n)}$ holds for n large enough

$$P_e^{(n)} \leqslant \inf_{\bar{\alpha} \in \mathcal{E}_R^*} 2^{-n\sum_1^k i\, m_i(\bar{\alpha})} \tag{4.49}$$

where $m_i(\bar{\alpha})$ is the stationary p.d. of $\Gamma(\bar{\alpha})$ and I_i is the I -divergence between the i-th row of $\Gamma(\bar{\alpha})$ and the i-th row of Π

<u>Proof</u> If condition (4.48) is satisfied, then $|\mathcal{B}^c_{n,R}| < |\mathcal{F}^c_n|$ and since $\mathcal{B}^c_{n,R}$ contains the sequences having the smallest $\mathcal{P}$ -probability, $\mathcal{P}(\mathcal{B}^c_{n,R}) \leqslant \mathcal{P}(\mathcal{F}^c_n)$ or also

$$P_e^{(n)} \leqslant \mathcal{P}(\mathcal{F}^c_n) \tag{4.50}$$

By (4.45) inequality (4.50) implies the thesis, since the non zero components of $\bar{\varepsilon}$ are arbitraryly small. Q.d.e.

<u>Theorem 4.2</u> If condition (4.48) is satisfied for some $\bar{\alpha}$, then the following asymptotic expression for $P_e^{(n)}$ is valid:

$$P_e^{(n)} \cong \sup_{\bar{\alpha} \in \mathcal{E}_R} 2^{-n\sum_1^k i\, m_i(\bar{\alpha}) I_i} \tag{4.51}$$

<u>Proof</u> It follows immediately from (4.42) and (4.49)

It should be remarked that in case $\mathcal{E}_R^*$ defined by (4.48) is not empty, then our problem is completely solved, as stated by Theorem 4.2.

It can happen, however, that $\mathcal{C}_R^*$ is empty. In other words it can happen that there is no $\bar{\alpha} \in \mathcal{C}_R$ for which $S(\bar{\alpha}) < R$. In this case we can introduce, along with the true encoding rate R a new encoding rate S , defined as follows:

$$S = \inf_{\bar{\alpha} \in \mathcal{C}_R} S(\bar{\alpha}) \tag{4.52}$$

Of course $S > R$ and therefore the set $\mathcal{B}_{n,S}$ made by the 2^{nS} most $\mathcal{P}$-probable sequences contains the set $\mathcal{B}_{n,R}$, and consequently

$$\mathcal{P}(\mathcal{B}^c_{n,S}) < \mathcal{P}(\mathcal{B}^c_{n,R}) = P_e^{(n)}. \tag{4.53}$$

Now we consider S as a new rate, and assigning 2^{nS} distinct codewords to the 2^{nS} sequences of $\mathcal{B}_{n,S}$ we get a new error probability $P_e^{\prime(n)} \triangleq \mathcal{P}(\mathcal{B}^c_{n,S})$ such that

$$P_e^{\prime(n)} < P_e^{(n)} \qquad \forall n \tag{4.54}$$

Of course at this point one can apply the previous considerations to $P_e^{\prime(n)}$ and get

$$P_e^{\prime(n)} \geqslant \sup_{\bar{\alpha} \in \mathcal{C}_S} 2^{-n\sum_1^k m_i(\bar{\alpha}) I_i}$$

where of course now $\bar{\alpha}$ must be in the set $\mathcal{C}_S$ and not in $\mathcal{C}_R$. On the other hand now

$$\left|\mathfrak{F}_n\right| = \left|\mathcal{B}_{n,s}\right| = 2^{nS}$$

and therefore inequality (4.50) is true with $P_e'^{(n)}$ instead of $P_e^{(n)}$:

$$P_e'^{(n)} \leqslant \mathcal{P}(\mathfrak{F}_n^c) \cong 2^{-n\sum_1^k i\ m_i(\bar{\alpha}^*) I_i} \tag{4.55}$$

where $\bar{\alpha}^*$ realizes the infimum in (4.52) and I_i is an I-divergence refferring to $\Gamma(\bar{\alpha}^*)$ and Π.

To summarize, the following inequalities to $P_e'^{(n)}$:

$$\sup_{\alpha \in \mathcal{E}_S} 2^{-n\sum_1^k i\ m_i(\bar{\alpha}) I_i} \leqslant P_e'^{(n)} \leqslant 2^{-n\sum_1^k i\ m_i(\bar{\alpha}^*) I_i} \tag{4.56}$$

Of course inequalities (4.56) do not imply much about $P_e^{(n)}$, but we could adopt the viewpoint of considering R as a "design encoding rate" and S in (4.52) as an " operating encoding rate", when $R < S$. If however $R > S(\bar{\alpha})$ for some $\bar{\alpha}$ in $\mathcal{E}_R$, the asymptotic behaviour of $P_e^{(n)}$ is described by (4.51), while if $R < S$ the relevant error probability is $P_e'^{(n)}$.

We observe that the exponents involved in our considerations about the error probability are weighted means of I-divergences; moreover in the memoryless case the true exponent is an I-divergence. This makes us consider as plausible the following conjecture on the true exponent in the Markovian case:

<u>Conjecture</u>: In the Markovian case the true exponent for the error probability $P_e^{(n)}$ is a weighted mean of I-divergences.

where the weights are the K components of the invariant probability distribution of a proper stochastic matrix , $\Gamma(\alpha^*)$ say, and the I-divergences are computed between the rows of $\Gamma(\alpha^*)$ and the rows of the original Markov matrix Π.

So far this conjecture has been neither proved nor disproved.

LITERATURE

[1] Ash, R., " Information Theory" , Interscience, 1965.

[2] Csiszár, I. and G. Longo, " On the Error Exponent for Source Coding etc." , Studia Scientiarum Mathematicarum Hungarica, 6,(1971), 181-191.

[3] Koopmans, L., " Asymptotic Rate of Discrimination for Markov Processes" , Ann. Math. Stat. 31, (1960), 982-994.

[4] Longo, G., " Source Coding Theory" , Lecture Notes, CISM, Udine, 1970.

[5] Longo, G., " On the Error Exponent for Markov Sources" Presented at the Second International Symposium on Information Theory, Tsahkadsor, U.R.S.S., Sept. 1971, To be published on " Problems of Control and Information Theory".

[6] Longo, G., " On the Error Exponent for Markov Sources" To be published in the Preceedings of the Sixth Prague Conference on Information Theory, Sept. 1971.

[7] Feller, W., " An Introduction to Probability Theory and Its Applications" , Vol 1, 3rd Edition, J. Wiley & Sons, 1968.

Contents

Printed in the United States
By Bookmasters